The Receiving End

The Receiving End
Consumer accounts of
social help for children

Edited by
Noel Timms

Professor of Applied Social Studies,
University of Bradford

Routledge & Kegan Paul
London and Boston

First published in 1973
by Routledge & Kegan Paul Ltd
Broadway House, 68–74 Carter Lane,
London EC4V 5EL and
9 Park Street,
Boston, Mass. 02108, U.S.A.

Printed in Great Britain at the
St Ann's Press, Park Road,
Altrincham, Cheshire WA14 5QQ

© Noel Timms 1973

ISBN 0 7100 7549 9 (c)
ISBN 0 7100 7550 2 (p)

Contents

1 Introduction 1

2 Adoption experiences 6
With a voluntary agency 6
With a Child Guidance Clinic 14
With a statutory department 17

3 Jane and Susan—an account of two adoptions 24

4 Recalling experiences at a child psychiatric unit 39

5 A children's home and a foster home compared 44

6 A children's home remembered 49

7 Fostering—the experience of a single woman 53

References 101

Introduction

This book is taken up with accounts that users of social service have given of their experiences in one or other of our social services. The services are concerned with children: an adoptive mother describes her application for a baby from a voluntary society and contrasts this with a second application to a local authority, also briefly describing her experiences with a Child Guidance Clinic; another mother describes two adoptions from a statutory authority; a nineteen-year-old girl recalls her year's treatment at a child psychiatric unit when she was twelve; two older adolescents discern some important features of their time in the care of a local authority; finally, a foster mother describes at length her experiences as both giving and receiving service. A range of agencies and a variety of problems are surveyed, but each contribution represents the user's view given entirely in their own words.

Social workers have for long thought of themselves as concerned with a user's view of the world. 'Start where the client is' has been a practical maxim that seemed to give effective shorthand expression to this concern. Recently, however, a number of studies suggest that whilst social workers may well have started where the client was, they failed to stay there long enough fully to appreciate what he was saying. The systematic study of what is termed consumer opinion has only begun in the last few years, but already interesting work has been undertaken. Nicholson (1966), for example, questioned users of Mother and Baby Homes in an attempt to discover opinion on the food, the comfort, the purpose of such organisations. In the field of the evaluation of the results of social casework, we can see a marked change between *Girls at Vocational High* (Meyer, Borgatta and Jones, 1965) which hardly referred to client perception of social work and the recent research by Goldberg (1970) on services for the old which devotes a chapter to a consideration of the views and appraisals of the old people who received help. Professionals and delinquents have been asked to evaluate professional methods of help (Gottesfeld, 1965); caseworkers and clients have been interviewed concerning purpose in casework (Schmidt, 1969); young people in a residential programme have been asked to assess the extent to which staff members could meet certain needs (Beker, 1965); adopters have been studied in connection with the services they received (Goodacre, 1966); patients have been interviewed in relation to medical social work help (Butrym, 1968); former users of a casework agency have described their experiences as clients (Mayer and Timms, 1970).

This suggests perhaps that we now have fairly extensive knowledge of the perspective of the user, but for a number of reasons this is not the case. In the first place it is not easy, especially for social workers who undertake research, to maintain a clear and systematic distinction between the views of the social worker and those of the client. Thus, in one of the studies mentioned above, the questionnaire administered to the clientele consisted of items drawn entirely from the opinions of the professionals concerned. The following passage from Schmidt (1969) shows how easily the clients' purposes become fused with those of the worker.

In using the term 'worker's purpose' there was no intention to disregard the client; the client's needs and desires were still the primary consideration. Rather, the theoretical assumption was that the worker articulates and helps to clarify objectives but the goals of casework are client centered; they evolve from a realistic appraisal of the client's problem and are continually related to his motivation, capacity, and objectives for himself as these are conveyed to and perceived by the worker.

Second, the extended exploration of the client's view of the service he has received raises a number of difficulties, of which limitations of language and the effects of relationship seem to be the most serious. Cohen (1972) has recently drawn attention to the difficulty users of a social service often experience in finding a language with which to talk about and to evaluate the social services. This is partly because the process of help is difficult to grasp and partly because a number of distinct activities are often grouped together under the single term 'the welfare'. Difficulties of relationship arise through feelings of indebtedness deriving from the reception of at least some friendly attention. Thus, it is not uncommon to hear of social service use such expressions as, 'They're very good, really'; 'They are doing their best; they cannot do any more.' During a recent study of Catholic Mother and Baby Homes when I was attempting to elicit 'consumer' response, one of the girls turned on the others in the group with the remark: 'What right have we to complain? Are we queens? We should be grateful for anything people do for us.'

Third, pressures of an organisational and professional nature may distort the voice of the client so that it simply echoes back whatever the professionals or the organisations wish to hear. As Oakeshott (1955) has written of this problem in its wider political context:

> It is safe to say that we, 'the people', never ask for what we have not been prompted to desire; we corrupt policy, not by our own shortsighted demands, but by our responsiveness to what is suggested and promised to us. Our voice is loud, but our utterance is the repetition of simple lessons well learned.

We are a long way from the solution of these and other problems that beset attempts to discern the genuine voice of

3

the client in the social services. The accounts presented in this book are a contribution to the continuing effort patiently to explore the meaning of service to the user. They are not part of a formal research project. Nor can we read them as accounts somehow of what 'really' happened. They show, simply and graphically, a number of people actively at work, responding to the service offered, and endeavouring to make some kind of evaluative sense of it.

This small collection of experiences will, it is hoped, reach a variety of readers. They can be used as a simple introduction for those who know little of the social services to some of the problems the services hope to solve. One account in particular (that of the foster mother) could well be read by prospective or actual foster parents so that they might helpfully anticipate and come to terms with similar or related problems. For readers with more knowledge of the social services and social work, the accounts raise important points of general and particular significance. We are shown, for example, ways in which taking help seems to carry important and usually not beneficial implications for the way in which clients think of themselves. Sometimes the implication is sharp but not of a long-term nature (as in the case of the young woman recalling her experiences at a child psychiatric unit), sometimes it is less easy to grasp and more pervasive. This aspect is further developed in other accounts which seem to throw light on the crucial importance of what social workers usually describe as accep-tance. This is clearly illustrated in the attempt of a former user to assess the relative merits of foster care and the children's home.

Students of social work and even experienced workers may find that these accounts present a challenge to constructive imagination as they endeavour to speculate on why these accounts are as they are and what kinds of intervention might have contributed to a different outcome. This book also helps us to grasp more sympathetically the problems that often face people who have the job of carrying out policies which in general seem sensible and beneficial. The story of Pam, for instance, shows in detail the difficulties of implementing the policy of encouraging contact between natural parents and their fostered children. Perhaps the kinds of difficulty described in this one instance help to explain the recent findings of George (1970) that the policy in question was rarely actively implemented.

These accounts, collected over a period of years, begin to tell one part of the complexity of giving and taking help. They show some appreciated and some not so useful social workers. They underline some simple 'home truths' about social work that are sometimes ignored by both practitioners and their critics. These could be listed in the form of some elementary rules: always explain your procedures, help clients (male as well as female) to acknowledge their feelings; remember that the client may feel and may be relatively powerless and that worker and client may not share the same time perspective; remember, also, that formal and informal sources of help usually co-exist in the same situation and that they may interact positively or negatively. But the interest of these accounts cannot be exhausted by the derivation of such maxims, useful as they undoubtedly are. As we read these detailed stories we can begin to see again some of the difficulties facing any explanatory theory used as a guide for social work operations. Perhaps we should envisage for such theory a rather modest role, analogous to that accorded by Aquinas to 'disquisitions on general morality', which, he suggests, are increasingly untrustworthy as we descend to the detail of individual cases.

> The factors are infinitely variable, and cannot be settled either by art or precedent. Judgement should be left to the people concerned. Each must set himself to act according to the immediate situation and the circumstances involved. The decision may be unerring in the concrete, despite the uneasy debate in the abstract. Nevertheless, the moralist [social work theorist] can provide some help and direction in such cases.

Adoption experiences

2

With a voluntary agency

At the time we first applied to the adoption agency we had been married for two years. My husband was thirty-nine and I was twenty-nine. I had previously lost an ovary through cysts so that the doctors were willing to investigate our apparent infertility more rapidly than usual. (They did, however, insist that I gave up my research which necessitated my travelling and living away from home part of the time.) We chose this agency partly because of my husband's religion, and partly because a friend, who was an Adoption Officer for a local authority, recommended them.

The agency's method was to carry out all the initial investigations by correspondence. We filled in questionnaires, sent medical reports and supplied references all without ever discussing adoption in any detail. I was surprised to find that they operated like this and I found it extremely unsatisfactory for a number of reasons:

(a) Because it was difficult to have to deal formally with unknown people about a matter which was so emotionally charged for us.

(b) Because they never explained their procedure to us so that we never knew what the next stage would be or how many more hurdles lay in front of us. We never felt we could ask about this which was probably rather weak-kneed of us, but we did feel so entirely in their hands and nervous about antagonising them in any way—after all, they had the babies! This

6

feeling of utter helplessness, to me at any rate, characterised our position and our dealings with adoption agencies both with our first and, less markedly, with our second child. After all, how many natural parents would take kindly to having their potential to be good parents assessed by someone who held the power to prevent them having a child? You have only got to listen to the uproar when someone suggests that there might have to be some statutory limitation on the size of families in future, to realise that the right to become parents to as many children as you choose is considered by most an unalienable right. Of course selection is necessary. I am not in the least arguing for indiscriminate acceptance of applicants, but only that those who undertake this very delicate task should fully understand the position that both they and we are in. They are not God, even if they are performing one of His functions, and they should not assume His infallibility. Just occasionally the client may also be right.

Another facet of the nervousness I felt in dealing with the agency was the fear of betraying anxiety and tension. Practically all the literature for intending adopters and for adoption caseworkers stresses the need for potential parents to be relaxed people; yet who can be really relaxed in such an anxiety provoking situation? There may already have been months, if not years, of frustration and disappointment. You know that the interview may be the turning point in this bitter cycle and all your hopes rest with the agency. I'm sure it is inevitable to feel at least partly that one is on trial. Can the interviewer discriminate between natural tension in this situation and a basically tense personality? I do not necessarily think so.

Perhaps another reason for not asking the agency details of their procedure is that one does not easily question someone from whom one expects and hopes for a great favour. One *wants* to think highly of them. I expected the agency to be understanding and helpful. Looking back, I probably thought they were always just on the point of revealing the future to us. One lives and learns!

(c) As they never explained their procedure we had no

7

opportunity to decide whether we were happy about accepting their regulations. I will go into this point in greater detail later.

(d) Because there was no opportunity to discuss our feelings about adoption with them. What are these 'feelings' one is meant to have about adoption?

I have thought long and hard about this and I wonder whether it is 'the lack of feelings that one normally expects to have about a new baby' that we adopters have to come to terms with, rather than anything more positive. I think this was basically how I felt. How do natural parents feel, particularly about their first baby? They have a strong desire to have the child of a beloved partner, to create together the embodiment of their love for each other, to give each other a child of their own. It is the ability to relinquish these ideals which is so hard for intending adopters, or at least, was hard for me. Then there are a whole new set of considerations in having an adopted baby which one has not normally ever thought about. I wondered whether I would be able to love a baby not born to me—I don't think there's any answer to this until you try it out, but assurances from other adoptive parents are helpful. I wondered whether, in some way, we were meant not to have children but to do something else with our lives. I wondered whether our relationship with our adopted child would ever be as complete and whole-hearted, on both sides, as that with a natural child. I wondered how our parents would take to the idea. I wondered how I would feel about the natural mother of my child—whether I would ever be able to stop worrying about her—and so on *ad infinitum*. Perhaps it is a good thing in a way that adoption is so difficult; for me at least it became such a totally desirable goal in itself that I stopped worrying about anything else! As it happened I had had many long discussions with the Adoption Officer friend and with several adoptive mothers and I think I had fairly well sorted out my own feelings, but I had mistakenly relied on the contact with the agency's worker to provoke my husband into discussing his feelings.

I should explain that my husband was perfectly willing for us to make the initial application but at that time he could not apparently see (his words: 'did not consider') that it needed discussion in any depth. This was in fact because although we had gone through the usual infertility tests and were thought to have less than average chances of conceiving I was still to undergo a ventro-suspension operation which might have helped, and he was convinced that we would conceive and thought of our application as an insurance against disappointment. When, after the operation (about three months after our initial application to the adoption agency), we were told that we were very unlikely to have a baby, he began to face the necessity of adoption and we were able to discuss our feelings in greater depth; but this was certainly not facilitated by the agency in any way.

We understood the need for a certain amount of the initial investigation to be done by correspondence as there were no local officers to visit us, but we would gladly have visited them if requested. On the credit side I think they were remarkably quick with the whole process and this is a great help when one has already undergone a considerable period of strain. We originally applied in May, our medical reports were held up because of my operation and because of a serious illness my husband had suffered in the past. We were visited in October and accepted officially a week later at the beginning of November. They always answered letters promptly. In January we were offered a baby whom we felt was not the right one for us—more about this later—and our daughter arrived in March. I think that less than a year from start to finish is probably fairly exceptional. I might add that we were also relieved that the agency were prepared to accept us despite my husband's medical record which included both tuberculosis and cancer, and that they did not insist—as I believe some voluntary agencies do—that one is more or less guaranteed never to have a born child.

When the agency's worker did finally visit us she spent about two hours with us and stayed to supper. We found her very pleasant and felt at ease with her. She was, I believe, originally an S.R.N. and had been doing adoption work with this agency for many years. She was second-in-command of the adoptions section. She spent quite a large part of her time with us asking a series of questions about such things as our backgrounds, families, education, qualifications, earnings, interests and so on, but never about our feelings about any aspects of adoption. Her questions seemed relevant but didn't go nearly far enough. She did say that they believed the child should be told about being adopted as soon as possible, in fact that it should never know a time when the first mention of adoption was made. She saw us together all the time, not separately, and she was shown round the house. Then she explained the agency's policy to us. One thing she told us was that my husband was only just within their age limits and would not have been accepted for a first child if he had been a year older. Then she told us that they always kept the babies in nurseries for six weeks before placing them with the adoptive parents—this meant six weeks with the natural mother then six weeks in a nursery, so that the child would be three months old by the time it was placed with us. I was frankly appalled at this information—and probably showed it. Erroneously, I had imagined that babies were placed with adopters as early as was compatible with the natural mothers' desire to care for them. I felt very strongly about this, partly because of my own wish to have a baby as young as possible—particularly the first— (and I must say that this is borne out by my experience with our second who arrived at the grand age of ten days), but also because, having read Bowlby etc., I was very concerned about damage to a child who was being moved twice and losing contact with a mother figure—both unnecessarily. I questioned the practice but our worker was adamant that a proper medical report could not be made on the child without a six-week stay in their nursery, and that this period also did much to ensure that the natural mother would not reclaim the child after it was placed in the adoptive home.

I spent the next few days hectically trying to collect evidence and opinions to support my own point of view—partly in an attempt to convince my husband that I was not being totally unreasonable. I don't think, at this stage, that he really agreed with me (his comment: 'on the grounds that the agency's experience in this field was long and considerable'). Nor, of course, was it any good trying to change the agency's policy. I remember feeling extremely resentful that they had put me in this position with my husband. If I remember rightly, we wrote one letter to them but they said in reply that we should change our agency if we could not accept their regulations— a course which was rendered virtually impossible by the length of negotiations already completed, the emotional investment, and the relative uncertainty, in view of my husband's age and medical record, of ever being accepted by anyone else. However, had we known their system earlier I think we would undoubtedly have tried elsewhere.

The method of actually placing the baby had been well explained at our interview. We were told that we would receive details of the baby by letter and that we would then discuss it on the phone. I found this a very satisfactory system— better than an initial phone call about a baby, when one tends to be so excited that one cannot take it all in. With the relevant information in front of us in a letter we could re-read it and it had a somewhat calming effect—proof that the baby really existed perhaps. The agency had nurseries in various parts of the country and we were told that 'our' baby might be in any of these and we might have to make a long trip. I think it was primarily for this reason that the agency's policy was for the baby to be brought home straight away. I thought at the time that this was preferable, and I think perhaps with the first it would have been very frustrating to have had to come away without the baby, but it certainly does add a large element of anxiety to the occasion—anxiety about whether one can take to the baby or not. This agency said that even if the baby were considerably older they would not agree to the adoptive mother staying near the nursery and visiting a few times so that the baby had the opportunity to make the change gradually—again I strongly disagreed with them, but by this time had learnt that it was no use saying anything.

In fact, we did not take to the first baby we were offered. We both found this an extremely distressing experience and the circumstances did not make it any easier. This baby had been taken home by the grandparents who then decided to let him go for adoption after all. Thus he was three and a half months when we went to the nursery and five months when he was offered for adoption. Although we were worried about his age we accepted that it was at least partly unavoidable. We were told that his background was an exceptionally good match with our own and that we might have to wait a long time for another as close. We had discussed 'matching' during our original interview and knew that the agency's policy was to attempt to match as closely as possible for colouring, educational background and interests of the natural parents. At the time we went along with this—agreeing that the child might feel happier if he was not subject to comments about his not looking like anyone in the family, and that it would be easier for him to grow up in an educational and cultural environment that would as nearly as possible approximate that which he would normally have inhabited. However, this is a counsel of perfection and although I think I basically still agree I certainly do not believe, as our worker did, that there is *the* right baby for each adoptive couple.

The worker made it quite clear that we must feel the baby was right and that we should not accept him unless we did. We went about two hours journey to see him and when we arrived at the nursery we were shown straight into the room where he was with other children and nurses all around, without so much as even the offer of the cloakroom. The worker, of course, was not with us. I was surprised at the complete lack of tact and perhaps they could sense our unease as we were then left alone with the baby for a short time before the matron came back to ask how we felt. Thank goodness we both felt the same—I think that was the only saving grace in the whole event. We were both quite shattered at our reaction, distressed for the baby and desperately concerned that we might not be able to

12

accept another baby either. The matron seemed condemning, and certainly there was no one who was at all helpful. As soon as we returned to London we rang the agency and, to give them their due, they were extremely kind and immediately assured us that we had done the right thing and it would not prejudice our chances of being offered another baby.

At this stage I think one of the major disadvantages of dealing with a national agency became apparent—there is no real support when things go wrong. I was extremely fortunate in having my Adoption Officer friend and a medical social worker, herself an adoptive mother, to turn to, because although our agency had been reassuring they either couldn't see that they had any part to play in the aftermath of what had been an extremely traumatic experience, or perhaps they didn't recognise that there would be any aftermath. What I needed then was someone to talk to and basically that was what these friends provided. My husband, once reassured by the agency, and of course immediately occupied again by a busy job, was rapidly back to normal; in any case he is not given to doubting himself. I, on the other hand, was full of agonising worries about whether I would be able to take to any baby at all, and these two friends were experienced enough to be able to reassure me again and again.

About two months later we received the letter about our daughter. We were immediately happy about her, partly because she was younger than we had dared to hope—only seven weeks. I still don't really know why this was except that her mother had kept her only for four weeks. I think the agency had let her go exceptionally early in order to satisfy us. In fact they said it was because she was so obviously developing and progressing well.

The placement was managed much more considerately this time. She was in the London nursery so the worker came herself and was there when H— was brought into the room. We were then left alone with her for a short while and then taken to see her little crib and to meet the nurses who had looked after her. I think all this was extremely satisfactory.

From the time the baby was placed with us I think the

13

agency handled everything extremely well. Admittedly they didn't visit us for ages but they were efficient about the adoption procedure and everything went smoothly. I had found that it was a disadvantage that they didn't necessarily have any direct dealings with the baby's natural mother as I should like to feel that they knew her, too. I felt that if they had known her personally and worked with her themselves they would have been far more sure that the decision she had reached about placing the baby for adoption was the right one for her, and that she was going to stick to it. I also felt extremely concerned for her and, in a way, involved with her and would have liked to know more about her personality, not just the factual information which could be passed through two third parties. I wanted to know how she was after the baby had gone. Also I am sure that the more of a 'person' she becomes to you, the easier it must be to talk to your child about her later on. However, the worker did go to considerable trouble to find out various things I felt I wanted to know and she did agree willingly to forward a letter from me to the baby's mother after the adoption order was made. We had a reply to this which I can give H— when she is old enough.

Another helpful practice was to give the adoptive parents a copy of a possible story one could tell an adopted child as it grew up to introduce the reality of adoption.

This is not really the end of our dealings with the voluntary agency but the rest belongs with our application for a second baby.

With a Child Guidance Clinic

Before we adopted our second baby we had a short period of contact with a Child Guidance Clinic. Our daughter was an extremely anxious and insecure child from the very beginning. She was delightful and we loved her deeply and she seemed happy much of the time, but she was obviously extremely alert and knew us and her own surroundings within days of coming home; subsequently any change in surroundings or change in the person handling her provoked an almost hysterical reaction. Loud noises terrified her. Men particularly, except her father and grandfather, appeared to frighten her and she cried bitterly at any new faces or any time I left her in a room on her own. She slept only lightly and woke at the least noise. All this of course made me anxious, too, and I am sure that to some extent I made matters worse by being over cautious. From the time she was eight months old her insecurity manifested itself in a form of masturbation which, as she grew older, became compulsive and almost continuous unless she was diverted by me. This meant a constant demand for my attention which competed with all the other demands on my time and left me, at times, in desperation. It certainly greatly detracted from my enjoyment of her and she may well have sensed this. Unfortunately her father's attitude was rather condemning and punitive so that many times I felt I was forced to stand between the two of them. I think that her relationship with him suffered considerably during this time but fortunately it has since mended. Also, of course, I lacked support from him in my own attempts to deal with the situation and was consequently less able to pursue a consistent course.

We first consulted our G.P. about H— when she was about fourteen months old. He was interested and always willing to discuss things but obviously knew very little about the matter. He did his best to be helpful and was to some extent supportive and reassuring to me but I gradually lost confidence as the situation deteriorated. He referred us to a paediatrician who was said to specialise in psychological problems, but he was quite useless. Eventually when H— was about two years old I asked if the G.P. would refer us to the local Child Guidance Clinic. He was reluctant to do so and told my husband that 'they are a lot of untrained women down there', which, since my husband was also not very enthusiastic about the referral, was most unhelpful. However, when I pressed him, he did refer us and was subsequently interested and impressed by the part they played.

I do not suppose we went to the clinic more than perhaps a

15

dozen times at the most. They were not totally helpful and I sometimes came away more depressed than when I went. Also, I was at times very frustrated because I felt that the P.S.W. was making wrong interpretations of things, or was quite impractical in her advice. But in general they were supportive and reassuring and this was basically what I needed. With their help I was eventually able to insist that H— attended a twice weekly playgroup which was a major factor in reversing the vicious circle we had got ourselves into. She made such a fuss that I am sure I would not have persevered without the Clinic's backing, and yet it helped her to gain confidence in her ability to be away from me for an hour or two and enabled me to complete some tasks without the constant tension and anxiety of her demands.

During the visits to the Clinic we discussed our plans to have a second child and what possible effect this might have on H—. This was, in fact, one reason I had wanted to go to the Clinic because I was very hesitant to put any further pressures on H— and also felt that, as things were, I would not be able to cope with another. I thought the P.S.W.'s attitudes to adoption were interesting—we had talked about adoption with H— as instructed by the adoption society (and as we felt was right) although I am sure that at this stage it meant nothing to her— but the P.S.W. was quite adamant that it was too early and that this was increasing her insecurity. She also felt that any talk of a little brother was going to have the same effect. Accordingly we did nothing further about our second application for the time being.

As things began to improve we started to think again about applying and the P.S.W. agreed with me that we should do this. Accordingly we applied to the voluntary society as before. Our application followed exactly the same course as before but of course we were not held up by medicals, so that the paper work was completed in about four months this time. In October the worker came to visit us. I was completely open with her about the trouble we had had with H— and about the action we had taken. She said they would need a letter from the Clinic and this I promised to obtain, but otherwise she did not seem too concerned. She did ask me if I still felt the same about the age of placing the baby, to which I replied that I did not have the same need for a very young baby but that I still felt the same about the principle of placing babies as early as possible.

Within a week or two of this visit I had obtained a letter from the Clinic which was, since the P.S.W. read it to me, a complete recommendation for the placement of a second child with us. I rang our worker to tell her that the letter was coming but was put through to the head of the section. Again being quite open, I gave a short explanation of why I was ringing. Her reaction was immediate and shocked: 'What a dreadful thing to do to such a little girl.' Needless to say we heard shortly after that that we had been refused for the second baby. To make matters worse they refused to give any honest explanation but sent a letter that said there was such a shortage of babies that we should be grateful to have got one. So ended our contacts with a voluntary adoption agency.

With a statutory department

Our application for a second baby was eventually turned down by the voluntary society from whom our first child had come. Needless to say we were extremely shocked—not the least because we had already got so far along the path towards achieving this baby after several months of references, medicals and other negotiations, and had begun to plan for him and to prepare our daughter for his arrival. Also this agency had stressed before placing our first child that they always preferred families to have two children, and that they would place any number once they had accepted your first application. Now it would be many more months, if not years, if we ever were going to have our second baby and the gap between the two children would be growing wider all the time. I remember that I felt again the same sense of desperation and complete helplessness that I felt during our first application and described

17

in that account. One is so completely at the mercy of other people.

Again, I was so fortunate in having a friend who was an Adoptions Officer with another local authority. I hate to think what happens to people who have no one they can turn to for advice. She told us that if we had been turned down by one voluntary society, especially one who had placed a child with us already, we were unlikely ever to be accepted by any other voluntary society. This information possibly saved us months of wasted time and bitter disappointment. On her advice we applied to our local authority, but they said they had closed their books—they omitted to tell us that it was only a temporary closure although I spoke to the Child Care Officer who had supervised our first baby and with whom I had always been friendly, and she was very sympathetic. I know other people who have been turned away for this reason only to hear later that someone else has been accepted, presumably just because they happened to apply at the right moment, and I am sure it would save much misunderstanding if the position was made quite clear.

We then applied to another local authority as a friend locally had adopted through them, and another friend had had two children placed with her by them and both were pleased with the way the children's department had dealt with them. But we were unlucky here, too, for they had made residence a qualification for accepting prospective adopters.

Finally, we applied to a third children's department. They didn't have a residence qualification, so that was a good start. As a result of our initial phone call they sent us a slightly off-putting circular letter which explained that they did not have many normal white babies but could help us if we were prepared to have a coloured or handicapped baby. We could easily have been put off by this as my husband was not happy about either, but I telephoned again and was told that it did not necessarily mean that they couldn't help us, but that it was a routine attempt to find parents for children who were more difficult to place. Anyway, we made a date to meet the Child Care Officer and she kindly agreed to go to my husband's office on that occasion because we were anxious not to raise any more false hopes at home.

It was extremely helpful to have this meeting right at the beginning of our contact with the children's department. I know I was very nervous but our worker, Miss M—, was very nice and helpful and friendly—I put some emphasis on her friendliness, which was always a feature of our relationship, because it was that which, more than anything else, made me feel that we were on the same side of the fence, so to speak. This is perhaps particularly important when dealing with a client who is, in fact, a member of the same profession. It is not pleasant even at the best of times to find oneself on the receiving end, and this was such a very dependent receiving end. This early meeting was also helpful as it provided the opportunity for us to tell her exactly what our position was and to outline our contacts with the previous agency, as indeed she explained that she would have to ask for their report, which we quite understood. At least we felt that she understood our point of view before she heard theirs. Finally, of course, the meeting also gave her the chance to explain exactly how their adoption procedure worked and this was most helpful as we then knew where we were throughout the negotiations. She explained that if they did turn us down she would hope to be able to tell us why, but that they had to reserve the right not to do so just in case there was some sort of medical reason which they could not disclose. We found this very reassuring. In passing I must say that I think it is an unwarrantable intrusion on civil liberties that our previous agency can and would give an adverse report of us to any other agency but that they are under no obligation to tell us what that report contains—it inevitably means that the applicant has no way of defending himself from what might be totally unjustified criticism.

The first meeting was followed by several other meetings with our worker—once she met my husband on his own and once or twice she came to our home during the day and met our daughter and me. Then she came home in the evening and talked to both of us. I really felt she knew us very well by the end of three months, which was about the length of time that these meetings were going on. At some stage during this time we also had medicals and our references were taken up. Miss M— explained that they would not ask for these formalities until she felt fairly sure that we were going to be accepted, which was very reassuring and sensible.

When Miss M— visited us in January she told us that as far as she was concerned our application was going to go through and that the Committee simply had to confirm it. This was great news, and on the strength of it I remember we asked if we would be safe in arranging a skiing holiday (for us and our daughter) in March. She said she thought not as, by mistake (not realising we still had to be confirmed by the Committee), we had already been allocated a baby who was, of course, not offered to us when the mistake was realised; but she thought that might be an indication of how rapidly our baby might arrive. In fact, through various administrative mix-ups, partly associated with the post-Seebohm reorganisation of their department which took place in January, and partly because of their Medical Officer's rigorous examination of our medical records on seeing our medical history, by April we were still waiting to be confirmed. I must say we did find this a great strain as we were very conscious after our previous experience that things can go wrong at the last minute. What made it worse was that Miss M— never bothered to let us know what was happening. To be fair I expect she was much too busy and did not realise we were worried. Dealing with a statutory children's department one has to realise that probably most of their other work is much more urgent, but it is not easy to appreciate this when one is feeling anxious. I know my husband's opinion of their efficiency went down with a bump. Eventually, however, we received official confirmation.

Sometime after this Miss M— and I met in her office to discuss very thoroughly what aspects of a baby's background we felt we could or could not cope with. Obviously some babies are born to extremely young mothers, or nothing at all is known about the father, or the parents are married yet do not want to keep the baby—all sorts of possibilities—but the only possibility which really bothered me was history of mental illness in the parents. I found it most sensible to have this discussion and I am sure it made the social worker's job easier too. Throughout our dealings with this local authority the most noticeable contrast between them and our original voluntary agency was their readiness to question their own methods. Miss M— frequently asked what we thought about things. She would say: 'We may be wrong to do it like this, what do you think?', or, 'We are trying this out. It may not suit everyone, but how do you feel about it?' It made us feel much easier, knowing that we did not have to fit into a tight mould.

In the summer I was offered the chance of doing a short piece of research which I could not resist, especially as we had no idea how long we might have to wait. So when our little son finally appeared at the end of September I was absolutely in the thick of it. I must say Miss M— was extremely under-standing about this—unlike the voluntary agency who had insisted that one gave up work from the time one was accepted by them. However, I remember our son's arrival as being frantic and exhausting. We were telephoned on Monday, went to see him on Tuesday in hospital where he was born—he was then seven days old and I was able to give him his bottle and hold him myself. Both Miss M— and the social worker who had worked with his mother came with us so that we were able to ask all the questions we wanted about his mother and his background. We had already agreed on the telephone that we were happy about him from what we were told then. Miss M—'s only concern was that he might turn out to be dark in colouring, but we fell for him immediately so it did not worry us in the least. On the Wednesday I had a long-standing arrangement to spend the day interviewing and there was nothing I could do to change it, so on Thursday we collected our baby and brought him home.

We had of course prepared our daughter to some extent for the new baby's arrival, but we decided not to tell her that he was actually coming until the Thursday morning or she would never have slept. For her this seemed to work very well and she was very happy and excited and rather over-awed by the event. We bought a little present for her to give him, and, unknown to her, one for him to give her which Miss M— kindly put in his carry-cot when she brought him out of the hospital. The fact that his mother's social worker came with us again was reassuring because I must say that although it was marvellous to have him straight from hospital so very young, I did feel very distressed while we waited outside knowing that his mother was saying good-bye to him. The fact that her social worker was there with her, and was able to tell us that her boyfriend (the father) was coming to take her back to her parents within the next few hours, was some help.

After A— had been placed with us I do not think the children's department played their part at all efficiently. When the initial six weeks was over they wouldn't let us inform our local authority for an extra two weeks because of some formality at their end, so we were late starting our probationary three months. At one stage they lost the mother's file and could not contact her and we were delayed again. There seemed to be one reason after another—partly, I realise, because their department was sorting itself out and everyone was taking on new roles and also, in their eyes, we were not an emergency—but we did not get A—'s adoption legalised until he was nine months old. Throughout this time I was surprised that Miss M— did not apparently realise that we might feel any anxiety. Some friends of ours who have adopted both their children from the same department experienced exactly the same sort of difficulty after their children were placed.

Finally his adoption went through. I must add that it was extremely helpful to our first child to be able to follow the adoption process right through. I think she understood what was going on perfectly well and found it very reassuring. Certainly, having a brother seems to have helped her to feel more secure. She is now happily settled at school, learning fast and rapidly becoming more outgoing. She still has some problems, but most of the time she seems a happy child. She is extremely fond of A— and in fact we feel that the four year gap is ideal for her. We have had virtually no jealousy, and they really enjoy each other's company. As for A—, he is totally gregarious, loves everyone, is extremely strong-willed and a thorough character. I don't suppose the effect of placing him at ten days is entirely responsible, but I like to think that the stability of his very early days has given him some of his self-confidence.

Jane and Susan— an account of two adoptions

3

David and I were married almost two years after our first meeting. The development of our relationship was slow and irregular. David wanted to be married, to have a home and, above all, a family, but nevertheless seemed reluctant to commit himself to a permanent relationship with me. He could only move forward by breaking off the relationship completely every few months, and then returning—sometimes within hours—as though nothing had happened. I had been quite sure of my feelings for him three or four months after we first met and found this ambivalence very painful, but not sufficiently painful to stop seeing him, as in spite of it all, I felt we were resolving something which had to be resolved if we were to have any future together.

A few weeks before we became engaged I had a very minor gynaecological abnormality which was treated surgically (D & C), and this opened up a good deal of discussion about our strong mutual wish to have children if we did marry. By this time we were in our thirties, but the gynaecologist assured me that there was no reason at all why I should not conceive, and that the D & C would actually increase the probability of this. A few months later we were married.

My failure to become pregnant was a terrible shock to me. I had always succeeded, and here was a situation completely beyond my control. The blow to my pride and self-esteem was shattering. I felt I had married David, whom I loved, under ¹se pretences, and felt guilty, angry, rejected, desperate—

and just plain sad. David was deeply disappointed, and depressed in an angry kind of way.

After a year we started investigations into the cause of our infertility. The first gynaecologist I saw clearly thought I was being very impatient, and made several references to a woman he knew who had had five children after she was thirty-seven, and was now 'sick of babies'. I sensed he had little real tolerance of failure. However, he referred me to the Family Planning Association, and the doctor there took me seriously. He did tests to show that David was fertile, and this was a tremendous relief to me, and he referred me back to the gynaecologist. He told me to 'come back in a year', but I said that I was too old to have that kind of time to waste. He admitted me and did another D & C and insufflation. A month later he said that although the investigations had revealed nothing he thought I 'would have to be patient'. I could not accept this, so he suggested adoption. I came home in a confused state of mind, and told David what he had said. He made no comment, and for a month we did not refer to the subject, but thought about it constantly. My work as an infants' teacher had brought me into contact with adopted children and their parents, so I was familiar with some aspects of adoption, but had never consciously related it to myself. However, during that month, it was not primarily the need to accept someone else's child which preoccupied me, it was the struggle to accept my own failure to give my husband the children he so deeply wanted. I think his problem was to accept my failure, and to start thinking about accepting someone else's child—and this was a new and alien idea to him. David is Welsh, and has very strong feelings about the continuation of his family line, and it has taken me many years to begin to understand the nature of this.

Eventually we were at last able to talk about adoption, but only after David had walked by himself across the moors for several hours, and decided that he wanted to stay married to me, and therefore we must consider adoption seriously if we wanted to bring up a family.

Full of hope, I at once wrote a letter to a national agency, giving outline particulars, including both dates of birth. They sent us an application form, which we completed in some detail, but eventually heard that our application was unsuccessful as they had such a long waiting list that we would have been over their maximum age limit before there was any possibility of a child being placed with us. We were very disappointed, and annoyed that they had not said this when I first wrote— they had wasted several precious weeks.

(Throughout the whole of the long process of infertility investigations and adoption procedures one of the most difficult things to accept was the general lack of understanding of the meaning of the word 'time' to people in our situation. Initially, there was the living from month to month: hope—disappointment—hope. Then the tests, which were tied to 'the right time'—waiting for appointments, waiting for letters, for telephone calls, for interviews and so on and on. Time assumes a disproportionate importance which has to be experienced to be understood, and from talking with other adoptive parents I know this is a common source of frustration. The general impression is that adoption workers, on the whole, are not sufficiently conscious of the feelings of hostility and resentment aroused by their disregard of the meaning of wasted time for applicants—feelings which can never be expressed, openly or otherwise, for fear of offending the omnipotent worker. There can be very few situations in which we feel as totally dependent on the skills and personality of the worker as in adoption work.)

After receiving the letter from the agency I spent a few hours wondering if we were, in fact, too old to adopt successfully. ʼried to weigh the evidence for and against as dispassionately could, and then telephoned an old friend with experience rking with children and whom I could trust to give an answer—in the child's interests, and not in ours. Her ʼ was immediate, 'No, of course you're not too old. Children's Department, they're much more flexible.' ʼe time she agreed to act as a referee.

We wrote to the Children's Officer, and had a formal reply saying that their Adoptions' Officer, Mrs E—, would telephone to arrange an appointment to come and see us. Two or three interminable weeks passed. I hardly left the house. At last the call came, and she arranged to come and see me two weeks later. I liked Mrs E— the moment I saw her. She was older than I was—very relaxed, very professional, and she was clearly in complete control of the situation. This gave me great confidence in her, which I never found to be misplaced. I felt we quickly established a good working relationship which enabled me to tell her freely about our marriage, our hopes, and our great disappointment in not having a family of our own. Her questions were shrewd, always relevant and reasonable, and I wanted to answer them as honestly as I could, which involved some heart-searching and self-revelation which she made much easier than I expected. She did not make an issue of our age, which was a relief to me, but spent more time on what my reaction might be if, after adopting a baby, we had one of our own, and how we might feel if our adopted children did not succeed academically. She asked what we would feel about a child of mixed racial parentage, what our attitude would be to telling the children about their natural parents and so on. I was able to tell her that David was deeply disappointed by our failure to have a child, and that although he said he thought adoption was the only solution I felt he was still very depressed about it all, and did not begin to accept it on any but an intellectual level. It was a very long interview covering a lot of ground, and Mrs E— left me with the feeling that we were in good hands.

Two weeks later she came again, primarily to see David, but in my presence. I sat back wondering how she would approach David, an interview I would certainly not like to have undertaken myself, especially complicated by the presence of a possibly critical third party. David was very tense, and clearly embarrassed by the whole situation. There was some general conversation, and then she said, 'Mr J—, are you as keen about adoption as your wife?' David said, 'No', and we all relaxed.

I was impressed by her skill. She grasped every nettle, and David's answers were frank, but I could see they were sound, and recognised how she was helping him to see adoption as something real and positive, and not just as an unwelcome fantasy. She explained the procedure to us, and told us when the Committee would meet, so that we had plenty of time for our medical examinations. She also suggested that it might be easier for David if we had a girl, as in her experience men with misgivings about adoption found girls easier to accept than boys. This proved a very wise suggestion.

Soon after the Committee Meeting we had a formal standard letter from the Children's Officer saying that our application had been approved, but reminding us that there was a long waiting list, and asking us not to keep contacting the department. Although we were delighted by the news of our acceptance, the impersonal and insensitive tone of the letter was rather chilling. However, we realised we must prepare for a long wait. I had already taken a supply teaching job but when this did not prove very satisfactory I asked Mrs E— if we could discuss our position on the waiting list. She readily came to see me and explained that although we had moved up the list since our application a few months earlier, there was such an acute shortage of babies that the list was now completely closed. It was going to be some considerable time before there was any hope of a baby so I found myself starting a new job; this was full-time teaching and I could hardly believe it was happening. It seemed like a retrograde step, but it was obviously realistic, and the job quickly proved both satisfying and enjoyable.

The months passed and I almost forgot about the baby. David and I never mentioned it and nobody else ever dared ˙ us about it. After Christmas, about a year after our first ication to the Children's Department, we both became very ssed. I was finding the travelling in the winter very tiring; had, inevitably, developed into a major demand, there y little energy over for social activities, and then—for time—I really believed I was pregnant—until our ʾe destroyed by a negative pregnancy test. At this point I began to feel we had made a terrible mistake. The right moment for adoption had been the previous summer, and that moment had passed. David's depression made it impossible for us to communicate, and I felt our marriage was threatened. I could sense his anger with me for not giving him a child, and recognised that things had gone too far for us to resolve the difficulties without help. The fact of recognising this, and the activity involved in organising some outside help was sufficiently stimulating to me to lift me right out of my depression. I had a single incredibly helpful interview with a psychiatrist who was very positive indeed about our prospects as adoptive parents, and he brought back the feelings I had had during the first months following our successful application. David went to a rather depressed psychiatrist who saw him weekly for a few months, but these sessions made very little impact on our lives.

In the spring I contacted Mrs E— again, and she herself raised the question of the long wait—now fifteen months. She thought it would now 'only' be another few months so at the end of August, exactly a year after taking the job, I left, feeling, I imagine, much as anyone feels when they finish work to have a baby. I was thinking of having a few weeks at home to make the final preparations, but after only two days Mrs E— rang asking if she could come and tell us about a baby girl who might be suitable for us. We heard about her, and gladly agreed to accept her. Her room had been ready for over a year, but lots of other things were needed, so at last I rushed out and bought everything. Two days before she was due to arrive Mrs E— telephoned; as soon as I heard her voice I knew the baby wasn't coming. The parents had decided to get married. I went to tell David and I felt that he was as shattered as I was. I felt I had lost the baby—that she had been mine, and had died. However, this setback had an extraordinary effect on David— from being very half-hearted about adoption he suddenly became very active. He telephoned me during the day with information about agencies from other areas prepared to consider outside applications, and in fact we actually applied to two other adoption agencies, involving us in more medical more references, and a whole flurry of activity which I found very embarrassing to explain to Mrs E—. I very strongly felt I wanted the baby to be chosen for us by Mrs E—, as I knew that no other agency could ever know us as well as she did. At the height of all this she telephoned to offer us another baby. My instinct told me this was not the right baby for us and David accepted without question the validity of my intuition, and so did Mrs E—. The weeks passed, and then the phone rang one evening, and David answered it. Some time later he came in and said, 'There's a baby girl who seems very suitable.' I rushed to the phone but heard nothing. I was so incredulous and overjoyed that in the end she was David's choice. During the next ten days I willed the telephone not to ring. After our experience with the first baby we decided that this time we would not tell a soul, not even our families. We were afraid to speak of it to each other. I aired the clothes and bedding secretly, and saw that the room was warm, but made no obvious preparations. Mrs E— had arranged to bring the baby on Saturday morning when David was at home. It was so foggy that I was sure she would never come and that, given the unexpected extra time, the baby's mother would change her mind. However, the sun came out, and at exactly the time she said she would come, Mrs E— arrived with our new daughter, aged six weeks. She gave us time to absorb her, and then gave us all the documents, and explained the procedures to us. David barely looked at the baby after Mrs E— left. I put her in her carry-cot in the nursery—a very self-possessed child, who seemed completely at home in her new surroundings.

David was very silent and preoccupied during lunch, and I started to give the baby her bottle he left abruptly nt for a long walk. My heart sank. During the afternoon back, and as I had to do some shopping for the baby m she was asleep in her pram in the garden, and left. ot back I found the pram empty, and the baby was h David who was completely at peace with her. the strain of the twenty-two months of waiting finally affected me physically, and I had a violent and pro-longed attack of vomiting. David took over the care of the baby, and by the end of the day she had become more his baby than mine. He had chosen her names, he had told people she had arrived—and his life had altered course.

Although Jane was only six weeks old when she arrived there were already signs of her very strong personality. She had no characteristics that seemed in any way alien to us. Each day strengthened our tie with her, and our deep conviction that she was the right baby for us. Our feelings of frustration and resentment about the long wait dissolved instantly—everything was vindicated by the arrival of Jane. Within a few days, however, we had our first visit from Mrs E— who came to see how Jane was settling down—and we really began to face the adoption procedure, and the fact that for the next three to four months her mother could reclaim her at any time. Every time the phone rang I became very anxious. Mrs E—'s second visit was unannounced, when I was out doing some Christmas shopping, and my mother was at home with Jane. It was a routine visit, but as I was seeing her to her car she casually mentioned that Jane's mother had not yet returned the document giving her consent to the adoption. I was stunned. I took my mother home and put Jane to bed in a trance. David came home and his reaction was similar. We sat in silence on the floor amidst all the unopened Christmas shopping the whole evening—just trying to prepare ourselves for life without Jane. In retrospect this seems to be an over-reaction, but during the whole of the adoption process, with both children, we found we had become hyper-sensitive, over anxious, at times quite paranoid, and quite desperately afraid that we might lose the children. Fortunately we never felt like this for very long, and the rest of the time we were overwhelmed by relief that we could love the children so easily, and probably happier with them than we had ever dared hope to be.

The morning after Mrs E—'s traumatic visit she rang first thing to say that the form had come in the post, and said that as soon as she had seen my face the previous evening she wished

31

she had never told me that it hadn't been returned, as it rarely did come back without some delay. In spite of our relief we began to feel our position to be precarious. I wrote all our Christmas cards without any reference to Jane, and then at the last minute, as she was still with us, added the news of her arrival. Christmas was wonderful, but we kept thinking of Jane's mother, whom we knew would be missing her very badly. Our compassion was mixed with fear that her unhappiness might precipitate some change in her situation, and for some days after Christmas I was particularly fearful when the telephone rang. Mrs E— came again, and then the Guardian *ad litem* visited us twice. The first time she came to see Jane with me and then went to visit Jane's mother in the evening. The second time she came when David was at home. I had told her all kinds of things about Jane and her development that I knew her mother would want to know, and in the return visit the Guardian *ad litem* painted us a vivid picture of Jane's mother and her parents, and some of this we will be able to pass on to Jane so that her first mother will seem a real person to her. We had known for some time the day of the court hearing, and it began to seem to me that there was no future beyond that date. The days before the court hearing were very ng. I began to count off the hours, until finally we met rs E— and the Guardian *ad litem* at the court. The proceedings ed exactly three minutes. When we came out we were too dazed to speak, but later I wrote to Mrs E— thanking her for her tremendous support during the two years since our first meeting. I had also written a long letter to Jane's mother who had said she would like to hear from me after the Adoption Order was made. I sent several colour photographs of Jane, and assured her that Jane would grow up knowing that her first mother had loved her enough to entrust her to us. This letter was sent by the Guardian *ad litem*.

The following day we applied to the Children's Department for a second child, and a month later heard we had been accepted by the Committee and placed on the waiting list, which was still very long. We then settled down to enjoy Jane, and for the first time in four years of married life we were not preoccupied with 'a baby' but 'our baby'.

We had hoped to have a two year gap between our children but David's job, as an engineer, took us all to London for a few months, and Jane was two years and three months when we returned. I had contacted the Children's Department telling them where we were going, and saying we hoped to have our new baby when we came back. The previous year Mrs E— had left. She had let me know she was leaving, and had told me again that there was a very long waiting list. On our return we wrote to the Children's Department and got a very impersonal letter saying that a new Adoptions' Officer would be coming at the end of the month, and that she would contact me by telephone when she arrived. After several weeks, having heard nothing, I telephoned Miss R— the new Adoptions' Officer. She apologised for not having contacted us, and we made an appointment for her to come and see me the following week. We arranged the interview at 1·30 p.m. as I knew that Jane would be asleep then, and that we would have about an hour in which to talk freely about adoption in a way that would not be appropriate in Jane's presence. Although she was not yet two and a half, Jane was a very mature child with a wide vocabulary and, I knew from experience, well able to understand much of an adult conversation. I knew she would listen with enormous interest to anything related to the longed for baby sister. Miss R—, however, arrived long after Jane was up—round about 3·45 p.m. She was a pleasant girl but I did not find her particularly sensitive, and she seemed uncertain about the whole interview. I had the impression she had looked at Jane's record before coming, but it was very clear that she knew very little about the agency, its procedures and policies, or about adoption generally. She stayed until 5·30 p.m., long after Jane's teatime, and she left me feeling uneasy and depressed. She had taken David's office telephone number and said she would telephone him to make an appointment to see him on his own, and in the meantime she would visit one of our referees. She did not ring David, but she did make an appointment to see one of the referees, but cancelled this a few minutes before she was due to arrive, causing some inconvenience and resentment. After a fortnight I left a message with her secretary to say that David would be very glad to hear from her whenever it was convenient. By return came a very cold letter, signed by the Children's Officer, saying that David had not been in touch with her as we had arranged and that our application must go before the Committee again. This letter came as a bombshell. I knew the misunderstanding about the phone call could easily be overcome but as the Committee had already approved our application for a second child our interpretation was that Miss R—, in that one interview with Jane and me, must have decided that we were not suitable. I was so angry, and so panic-stricken that I hardly knew what to do first. My real fear was that the agency's policy might have changed, and that they were no longer as flexible about upper age limits, or that possibly the Committee was now asking all applicants who had been waiting more than two years to apply again. I could not understand why we had not been told this by the agency at the time the policy was changed, or when I had telephoned to say that we would be away temporarily, or when I had written saying we were now ready for our second child, or by Miss R— herself when she came to see me. I felt very hostile towards Miss R— but obviously this had to be concealed which went very much against the grain. David telephoned her, and went to see her the same day. I begged him to try and be nice to her. We had far too much at stake to be able to afford the luxury of plain speaking—or so we thought at the time. For the first time in my life I really knew what it felt like to feel helpless in the hands of a social agency, and to be dependent on the goodwill and competence of a social worker in whom I had so little confidence. I had never felt this with Mrs E— once I had met her. She had treated us as I imagine she treated all her applicants—as worthwhile people involved in making a very important joint decision, and she had conveyed this to us by keeping appointments punctually and by coming to interviews prepared with all the necessary information. Our confidence in her was such that David was heard to say reassuringly to his parents before Jane's arrival, 'We know we'll have the right baby for us because we have such a very good adoption worker.'

David's interview with Miss R— was brief and uneventful. He described her as 'a bit scatty' but he was clearly much less threatened by the whole situation than I was. The next step was a joint interview, and she came to see us at home. Jane was very much in evidence again, but this interview was more relaxed, as I had David's presence to support me. She explained that the agency had changed their policy, and all applicants who had been on the waiting list two years or more had to apply again. We had to have more medicals, X-rays etc., but eventually we heard that we had been accepted again—the same letter from the Children's Officer. We gathered from Miss R— that there might not be a very long wait, so had a holiday. Soon after our return I had to go south and help look after a sick relative. Jane came with me, and we became so involved in our busy life there that it was a shock when the telephone rang one afternoon and there was Miss R— offering a baby girl who sounded just right. David was at the other end of the country. I telephoned him but he was in the middle of a meeting and said he would ring me that evening on his way home. He rang from a call box at a motorway service station—it was very noisy at his end, and I did not want to raise my voice so that any details about the baby's background could be overheard. David said she sounded fine and we'd better accept, so I rang Miss R—. There was very little opportunity to think about the baby, and when, a few days later, Miss R— rang again to say that we could see her the next afternoon if we wished, I had to say it would be quite impossible for either of us. I have never ceased to be thankful that we were not able to see the baby. I thought things over and decided that it was time for me to take Jane home so that we had a few days on our own before the new baby arrived, and that this had become more important than any help I could give where I was.

Miss R— said she would bring the baby at midday, so I

suggested she had lunch with us as I knew it would be impossible for us to complete all the formalities and feed both children in less than two hours. David took a day's leave, and Jane and I enjoyed getting everything ready for the baby. We were looking out of the window by 12 o'clock. At 1·30 p.m. we were very depressed, with a tremendous feeling of anti-climax. We felt the only explanation was that she had confused the day. I was almost overwhelmed by weariness at the thought of having to go through it all again. Sadly we ate our lunch, and at 2 p.m. she arrived having been 'held up'. She had not telephoned in case hearing her voice had made us think she wasn't coming. David and I looked at the baby who was only a month old. She was very plain and covered in spots. Neither of us warmed to her but agreed with Miss R— that she was a very nice baby. After Miss R— finally left at about 4 p.m. David and I looked at each other in horror, and David said maybe we could change her for a boy. She cried a lot, and Jane asked when she would be going back with the lady. It was just about the worst day of my life. I didn't think I could ever love this child in the way I loved Jane. I felt that the realistic thing to do was to face up to this at once, and send her back because it was quite immoral to condemn her to a life as second best child. On the other hand, I argued to myself, how could we reject her, and the young mother who had allowed her to come to us, sending her with baby clothes she had obviously struggled to make herself, and she had even sent a present for Jane. The conflict kept me awake. I was in the same room as the baby so that I could feed her without disturbing anyone else. As I was feeding her I began to remember friends who had admitted not being immediately drawn to their own children, but of course for them there had been no question of sending them back. I began to feel better about her, and she certainly seemed a very contented and peaceful child. Even her spots, which were due to being overdressed in hot weather, seemed to be fading. Next morning she had her first visitors, who were full of admiration, and by the end of the day Susan was as much part of our lives as Jane. She was a very much easier, and more rewarding, baby as she always enjoyed her meals, and within three weeks her face had changed completely and by any standard she was, and still is, a beautiful child. A friend who is herself an Adoptions' Officer rang me shortly after Susan's arrival, and when I told her that we hadn't taken to Susan immediately she said at once that this was a very common reaction to a second baby, especially where there had been a very successful first adoption, as with Jane. She said she had considered whether to warn me in advance that this might happen but decided against it.

Miss R— paid her first visit unannounced, and her second by appointment, but she cancelled this half an hour after she was due to arrive. By this time I had adjusted to her unreliability, and as I was so relieved, and completely happy with Jane and Susan, I felt very forgiving. She then handed me on to the Guardian *ad litem* who arrived unannounced at lunchtime when the house was full of people. I said there was so much that I wanted to tell her about Susan so that she could give this news to her mother and father, so she agreed to come back later the same day, before going to see Susan's mother. The interviews with the Guardian *ad litem* again made us very anxious about the possibility of losing Susan. This time we felt it would have been even more devastating now that Jane was involved, but the weeks passed and eventually, with the minimum possible delay, Susan's Adoption Order was made. As we left the court I thought to myself that at last we were free to lead our own lives with Jane and Susan.

Jane is doing very well at school—all her reports have commented on her happy personality and her lively imagination. She has always had a good understanding of what it means to be adopted and this never seems to have presented any problems to her. She has seen the outside of the hospital ward where she was born, and this had great significance for her as it is something which the children have talked about at school and she did not have to feel excluded or different. We often talk about 'the foggy day when I came to live here', and so far nothing has happened to turn adoption into a stressful subject for any of us. Susan is now at nursery school three mornings a week. She also has a very strong personality but is much less mature emotionally than Jane was at the same age. She is very active and at school they think she is highly intelligent. She is very affectionate, very generous, boisterous but very lovable. I don't think she realises she is adopted, although I have told her the story of the day she came but she didn't want to listen. However, she was interested to see where she was born, and she is developing much more rapidly now, so I am beginning to look for opportunities to make her more aware of what adoption means.

David and I both feel that the children are all, and much more, than we could ever have hoped for. We are sure we could not love them any more if we had produced them ourselves, but at the same time we both wish that these two same children had been born to us instead of being adopted by us. The whole experience has left something rather like an old surgical scar—it is there, if you look hard enough, it doesn't hurt unless something knocks against it; and it's a very salutary reminder of what might have been if we had not had the stamina and motivation to embark on the long, slow process of adoption.

Recalling experiences at a child psychiatric unit

4

I was having problems at school at the time. I think I got too overwhelmed with certain lessons. If I didn't like them or even if I didn't like the teachers, I'd worry myself silly about those particular lessons and wouldn't think about the lessons that I enjoyed. I used to dread these lessons and it spoiled the whole week for me. I never could get down to revision for a lot of subjects at once and I think it was this that also worried me. Every time I went to the lessons, and especially double lessons, you got a lot of work and a lot of homework and I used to think, oh I've got all this to learn at the end of the year, for the exams.

In the second forms, obviously, you are doing a complete syllabus, you are doing a lot of subjects, and it sort of over-powered me; all this work to learn and I think that was at the back of my mind all the time, and so it got to the point that I stopped going to school, for a while anyway.

It was just after the Christmas holidays. I always hated going back after the holidays. It was just like a great big Monday, going back after Sunday. I wanted to leave school altogether. I think it was before this that I'd changed schools and it took me a very long time to get used to new friends and new teachers. Some of the teachers were very nice. The Headmaster was ever so nice. He had me into his office one day and we had a talk about school. He gave me suggestions as to how I might ease the work a little bit. This was the only time I saw anybody about the problem before going to see the psychiatrist. It was the Headmaster who pushed me into having Monday afternoon off so that I could go to the psychiatrist. He was all for it. He wanted to make sure I was having the best possible treatment. He was very understanding. I had been seeing my G.P. for a while before. He had talked to me a bit and he had prescribed some tranquillisers, but he did not have much chance to talk to me. Actually, though, it was a help even just to have that short talk. It gave me some point of the day to look forward to when I would be talking to somebody outside the family. I think that this was what I wanted. Come to think of it, I must have been going to see the G.P. some time before I went to see the psychiatrist.

Now when I went to see the psychiatrist I think I was a bit hurt, a bit put off the first time I saw the name of the psychiatric unit over the doorway. I was a bit upset about that, but as soon as I got to know that it was helpful I changed my opinions completely. I didn't tell the other girls I was going. When I told them I think they felt a bit sorry for me, that I'd had to go, but they didn't make fun of me or anything. I think that what I was frightened of to start with was I didn't want it spreading around that I was a bit funny, but they accepted it.

Of course, it's quite a long time ago, but I remember one time I went especially plainly. It was when Dr A— got a sort of box out, and she asked questions and I had to put the answers in appropriate slots. I can't remember exactly what I did now, but I felt as though I had been doing something for a change and I got a clearer idea of my family somehow, because she had been asking the sort of question where I sort of analysed my feelings towards my family. I felt as though I'd learned something in a way, from just being there that one afternoon, but I think I appreciated going each week. This regular meeting with somebody who wasn't the family, somebody I could still talk to personally. It eased my feelings, I could relieve my mind of problems.

For a long time my mother used to come with me. To start with I was glad that my mother went down with me, I was nervous about anything out of the ordinary and I was worried about it beforehand. I think my mother was a comfort to me to start with, somebody to talk to on the way down and on the way back again. At the same time I didn't want her to feel I was a burden. She couldn't get anything done herself all afternoon, with just being sat there, so I think I was pleased that she was having the social worker to talk to as well. My mother was going through a bad time as well, because she was getting worried about me being upset and I think it was a help to her as well to see the social worker. I think I felt pretty certain that it was all confidential, but I don't think to start with I liked to say too much because I just wasn't sure how much is talked about afterwards. But, as I got used to going I got to know Dr A— and I started talking more about personal things and I felt it was a help, I could talk quite freely. After my mother had been going for a while, I think she got a bit fed up and so Dr A— suggested I should go on my own. I'd never really thought about it in that way, just going by myself but when I did have time to think about it, it sort of suddenly felt like an adventure. I was going somewhere, and it was going to be a help to me, and going somewhere on my own. This was a sort of achievement at the end of the day. I would go back home again and I'd done it all by myself.

It was a regular Monday afternoon meeting you know. In a way I got to look forward to it, I didn't mind Monday mornings so much, knowing that I would be able to discuss my problems. I don't like Monday mornings somehow. Sunday nights even now I still worry about even though I don't know what's coming at work now. Before, when I was at school, I got so that certain lessons that I didn't like I'd dread them coming. Monday mornings especially, I used to hate these. So some Sunday nights I'd find myself lying awake for quite a while, but I think while I was going to see Dr A—, I didn't mind Monday mornings because I knew it was only half a day, and then I'd be away again and then once I'd got Monday over, the rest of the week wasn't so bad anyway.

After I began to see Dr A— it became easy to go back to school. Every time any problems did come up at school, I'd got somebody to talk these problems over with and that became easier. I still had one or two little cries to myself. I looked forward to going on a Monday to see Dr A— and then Tuesday morning would be a sort of a let-down. On Monday morning, I wouldn't mind my lessons, I'd get on with them because I knew I was going to see Dr A— so that any problems that I'd thought about I'd have somebody to talk to in the afternoon. Then on Tuesday mornings somehow it's, oh I've got another week before if anything crops up. I got very dependent on Monday afternoons to start with. It got easier later on and I felt that I was getting so that I could cope with things better myself. But at first I got very dependent and it was such a let down afterwards. I would really have liked more frequent meetings in the beginning, perhaps shorter but certainly more of them. Of course, this would break into all sorts of other things, other lessons, but looking back I would have liked shorter meetings more often.

After I'd been going every week, we got down to going once a month. Then we stopped and I went again two or three months later. Dr A— suggested that unless I started feeling depressed again it was probably alright to stop going and I think this was how it came up. She'd spread the visits out gradually so that they were less frequent and I was less dependent on going. I think I was a bit let down to start with, but on the last visit, after there had been such a gap since the last visit I got so that I accepted it. I felt it had been a great help and I could look back then and think how different I felt before going. I did not get much notice that it was going to end. I expect I would have probably clung on to the last time a lot more if I'd known. On the other hand she didn't say it suddenly, right we'll stop this time, it was sort of a suggestion, would I feel it would be alright to stop. If it comes out gradually like that, I accepted it. It was as if she had said if I wanted help, she was still there. But I was well enough to carry on on my own and I think I felt pleased with myself about that. It was after seeing Dr A— that I started making friends at school. It all started coming right together. I'd started talking to Dr A—, so I was talking to somebody who'd started off being a stranger and I suppose I felt, well among these other strangers, there must be somebody who's as easy to talk to. From there I found people I could tag on to, and gradually we became good friends, and we stayed friends through, well into the sixth form.

A children's home and a foster home compared 5

I was thirteen when I was taken into care. Some arrangements had already been made and I knew what was going to happen to me.

I was first admitted to the County Reception Centre where I stayed for a month, and I was boarded out after an introductory period of two weekends and a half-term school break. When the placement failed, I was re-admitted to the Reception Centre and transferred after another month to a small Family Group Home.

My foster parents had two sons of their own, one aged twenty-one and one a year younger than me and a year below me at school. They also had another foster daughter, she was eighteen and had been living with them since she was fourteen. It was with these last two that I had the most contact and it was they who mostly influenced my feelings whilst I was actually with the foster parents. Towards the young son I was jealous, I think I was rather sensitive while I was there—I watched him very jealously to see whether he was given any special privileges if I wasn't and if he received any preferential treatment. It was the same with the foster daughter, too, but not with any real feelings of jealousy, I think it was mostly because I didn't feel very secure there. I couldn't really understand why they wanted me and I didn't really see any reason why they should put up with me. Unfortunately there was nobody with whom I could talk, and nobody that I could easily tell that I was not really happy there, and I didn't really feel I fitted in with the atmosphere of the place. The Child Care Officer is theoretically the person to whom you are supposed to be able to talk, but I think I saw her, at least three different 'hers', at the most five different times while I was in care and I don't think I ever saw her alone.

The most striking feature of the boarding out was the loneliness, I was one child, a stranger with a family. The family had been going on for years and could not really be expected to adapt itself to me, and yet I was not old enough to adapt myself to people—not really. It was rather like a tug-of-war—and in turns they expected that, 'I am doing so much for you, surely I deserve something in return!', and that something in return always seemed to be far more than I could give. My loyalty—it couldn't be turned swiftly like that in a couple of months from one family I had just left to another family that I was just getting to know and yet it was expected of me, and I had to be on my best behaviour—there was no room for moods and tantrums. I was a visitor in the house all the time—I always had to make my own bed, even though I was late for school. I wasn't quite the daughter of the family and they were not really getting paid enough money for looking after me—I know that all the time I never really was their daughter, I was always their foster daughter and there was a feeling of indebtedness towards the family and towards the people who were responsible for putting me there. So many people seemed to be working towards my happiness that it was sacrilege to even suggest that I wasn't happy. You couldn't be unhappy in a foster home because the foster parents wanted you—they were trying to make you happy—the Child Care Officers were trying to make you happy—the people from the Homes were hoping that you were happy—everyone was hoping that you were happy. You had to be! There was no room for unhappiness and no one would admit that you could be unhappy because everything was so perfect. I think it is expecting an awful lot for fostering to work. People automatically think that the child will behave and react as their own, but there isn't the close bond between them, there is always the feeling that—I think

45

there must be—'Why should I look after this child? Why should I have the infinite patience that it needs—this isn't my child, it is somebody else's child and it is their fault that this child is in care? Why should I be the one who should have to bear it? Oh! I asked for it, I admit, but why should I really have to put up with this thing that they have given me?' And then I, as the foster child, have the feeling that these are not my parents—'Why should I do as they say? Oh! They look after me, they must have wanted me; they must have applied for it and they got me. It's not my fault that they got me; I didn't want to come here. Nobody asked me what my feelings on the subject were', and that, too, is one of the noticeable points about the whole business. While I was in the Reception Centre when I had been with the foster parents for the two weekends, I was asked, 'Did I enjoy it? Had I liked being there?' They knew that I knew that the idea was that I should go and stay with them, but I had to give the answer that was expected of me, 'Oh! We had a lovely time (for the weekend). It was gorgeous. I was spoilt and petted and fussed over and all I had to do was wash up and everybody was happy in showing me what a nice place it was.' But really, after two days you can't get a good idea of what a place is like and with a Child Care Officer that you don't know very well and the whole set up that you are not familiar with at all, you just had to give the answer, 'Yes, I liked it because you arranged it for me and I did as I was told', and so I said therefore, 'Yes, I liked it.' It was more or less up to me to say yes.

I went—it was on my shoulders—really the whole thing was very 'hit and miss'. I think the sky would have dropped in if I had dared to say no, I didn't really like it and what are you going to do about it? It must be awfully difficult for the foster parents' own children—they must be continually anxious and alert wondering if this peculiar person that has been put into my home and disrupted it and pushed me out with my parents —Is he or she going to be given anything I'm not going to be given? Is she going to be spoilt more than I am going to be spoilt? Gosh! I don't like her very much and she has got in the way, I know that I felt the same way about my foster mother and it is quite true that the parents can't avoid giving their own children little bits of extra. It might be quite calculating and to reassure them that they are still loved. It is so obvious to the foster child that they are the ones that don't fit in and they are the ones that feel that they have got to do the hard work and to change themselves to fit in with the family and the family are such a tight circle you have to work so hard to get into it. It is rather like an exclusive club. They can't avoid giving their own child some extra privileges so obvious and so obvious to me and I was so jealous—and really it was the worst possible thing that could have been done and yet it was so unavoidable.

I can't think why there is so much controversy about foster parents versus Children's Homes, Institutions versus foster parents—there is no comparison. In a Children's Home there is nothing except good behaviour demanded of a child—no loyalty and they don't have to fight their way into the circle— it is accepted on its own terms. There is no fighting inside the family circle, because each child is there on its own merits. No one has more right than another, there is no feeling that you have to be loyal to the houseparent and forsake your own. It is a neutral sort of place where you can go and recover from whatever has happened to you or get ready for the next step— Gosh!—there is no comparison at all between Homes and foster parents. I was infinitely happier in the Reception Centre and in the Family Group Home and given a choice I would never have gone to foster parents, a Children's Home was there specially for the children and there was no doubt about whether you are wanted or not or whether you fit in or not— it doesn't matter—it's just a choice place on earth because you know that they have got to look after you and all you have to do is behave yourself and that is not difficult. Of course there is no doubt that if it could be guaranteed to work, there is no doubt that the child would fit in and a magic word could be said— nothing would be better than the family situation. In a Children's Home there is always the feeling that I have not got a proper mummy and daddy, I have not got an ordinary home to go back to. I live in a Children's Home and that makes me a little bit different, but advantages far outweigh the disadvantages and you are free from the eternal questioning and 'Am I wanted?' 'Am I being good?'

A children's home remembered

6

The children's community home is set in a lovely part of the world, and it is here that I spent almost five years of my life, together with my brother Peter. I was eleven years old at the time.

The day that everything started to happen seemed like any other day except for the fact that we hadn't seen our mother for the last few days, not knowing she was in hospital. We had all been evicted from our flat a few weeks previously and had been staying with friends. The situation wasn't a very good one as it meant our missing school so that we could go with our mother to find another flat. We had been unlucky so far and at that particular time were staying with friends. My half-brother Paul then took us in hand and decided to seek advice and we found ourselves in a rather bleak building, being asked all sorts of questions as to how we had spent the last few weeks. What made it worse was the fact that Paul had to return to work almost immediately and it was very frightening being left alone not knowing what was going to happen to us. Being the eldest I tried to reassure my brother that everything would be alright eventually, although I hadn't a clue as to what it was all about. We were taken out for a meal, which was very welcome. It wasn't until late afternoon that we were told where we were going to spend the next few months, as it happened it was years rather than months. The description of the Home sounded very nice and at first we both took to the idea of going there, and it wasn't until we had actually left London that I realised what had happened. We were going to a completely strange place, strange people. We had been told that it would be for our own good and this we couldn't dispute. We had no choice. It would have been nice to have known that our mother had wanted it to be like this but that wasn't possible.

We arrived in the evening, it was the middle of January and a very dark, cold evening. The first thing that startled me was the size of the place and the iron gates which were still in place then. We were taken to the office first and it was here that the Child Care Officer who had brought us left, saying he would come and see us again very soon. We were introduced to a lady who told us where our mother was and that as soon as she was well she would come and see us. At that time I can remember thinking that when our mother did come, she would take us home with her, but this was not to be.

We were taken to one of the large houses, met our new 'housemother' as she was called, and so began our stay at the Home.

The next few days gave us the routine of what life was going to be like. We started at the junior school. Then the house we were in split up, the children going to various other houses, and we found ourselves in a quite different house from the first. Instead of a large, almost empty home, we were in a warm, friendly place, nicely decorated and filled with children which seemed to radiate a much happier atmosphere and we were glad we were there.

I started at a secondary school which I rather liked and during my time there I made a lot of friends, in fact I made more friends at school than at the Home. This was because I suppose I didn't really think I would be at the Home for very long and didn't really want to become involved too much. My brother, on the other hand, made a lot of friends at the Home mostly through joining the football team for which he still plays.

As time went by, and I realised that going home straight away wasn't going to be as easy as I had hoped, I resigned myself to the situation and decided to devote all my time to

A children's home remembered

studying in the hopes of getting a fairly good job when I eventually started work.

The Child Care Officer came to see us, and my relationship with her was fairly good considering the number of times she came and the length of time spent talking in private. I wanted to know so much, why we had to stay so long, how my mother was coping. The answers I received were adequate but then she would go into 'conference' with the housemother and I would think she was keeping something back from me. We became more friendly after I left and she would sometimes meet me in my lunch hour from work. I quite missed seeing her when she left to start a family of her own.

By this time I was nearing the end of my school days, and I got the opportunity of staying on for a further year to take a commercial course which would enable me to learn shorthand and typing. I felt this would be a great help in years to come and happily everyone agreed that I should take the course.

Before I actually left the Home, I started to spend one evening a week with my mother, I suppose to get to know her which I thought rather funny at the time but in actual fact it was very much a reality because when we met, we had virtually nothing to say to each other. I had received a fairly good education and had tried to better myself and had changed quite a bit from the young girl my mother had known. All the time I had been thinking of myself, what I was going to be like when I left, how I was going to cope, what I hadn't realised was how all this had affected my mother. I got the impression that she felt very guilty about Peter and I living where we did, so much so that whenever she came to visit us, she would wait outside the main entrance for us, as on her first visit she had taken us away from the house and all the other children had stood and watched and waved us good-bye. She felt she couldn't go through that every time she came, and to an extent we understood how she felt. Whilst we were at the Home, my mother had been staying in a hostel, a place we visited on a few occasions, rather like a prison, each person having their own very small room. I always felt very sad when I saw her there because she had so very little and I was enjoying good food and clean clothes. Those days spent with her made it startlingly clear what it was going to be like when I actually left, and it was with a great sense of sadness that I went to live with my mother, leaving behind friends and security, to go again to a strange new home.

My new home was a double room which I shared with my mother. For the first few weeks it was terrible, I was very unhappy. As both of us were at work all day, the evening became a routine of having a meal, clearing up and going to bed. Peter would come occasionally to see us, but in one room it was very crowded, and he always seemed a bit relieved when it was time to go.

When I look back, I am grateful for all that was afforded to me at the Home. My mother too, is grateful for all they did and together we have learnt to accept things as they are. Working here as I do and my brother's connections with the Home, hearing about old friends, I doubt very much if I will lose touch with the Home, unless my husband and I acquire a house (in the not too distant future I hope) far away. I hope I shall never forget my years at the Home.

Fostering—the experience of a single woman

7

I am writing this introduction many months after finishing the story of Pam. Having read the story again recently I think it is only fair to all concerned to explain one or two points that come to mind in the light of more experience, and consequently more understanding.

I see that some of my views of Children's Homes as we know them today appear to be very critical, and I have given very few constructive suggestions. I have seen and experienced the faults, and they really do exist, but I have every sympathy with those trying to make improvements in this direction. It is an impossible task.

I think I should also explain that I did not write this story as a review of the situation at the end of two years, but based it on notes I had kept from the very beginning. I kept these notes initially to help myself as, being on my own with Pam, I found I had no one to turn to over each little difficulty, as even my family and friends, although concerned and interested, could not put themselves into my place as they had never had experience of this sort of thing before; so, rather than bothering the Child Care Officers over every little crisis that arose, I expressed my worries in writing and this was a tremendous help However, it does mean that the story as it stands now was written in the light of the knowledge I had at the time; as each new aspect came to light, so I included it in the story. Had I had greater understanding from the beginning, no doubt I would have acted differently on many occasions, but I am sure this 'working in the dark' must be the experience of all foster parents.

One of the things that I see so differently now is the striking difference in our backgrounds. I thought I was relatively broad minded when I started, having already had some experience of working for a short while in a Children's Home, apart from the many visits to others, including Pam's, but I can see now that my very 'middle-class' upbringing so affected my judgments that some of the petty situations arose purely as a result of this and many of the ups and downs we had were conditioned by what I called 'normal' ways of going on. Mind you, I do sincerely believe that many of my feelings over this were not so much for myself, but for the neighbourhood in which we lived. For example, the obscene swear words did not worry *me* particularly—I certainly didn't use them, nor did I encourage her to—no, my fear was that she would be rejected by the society in which we lived, and my fears were well founded, as you will see. Of course, a way around this would have been for me to live in her own home area, but let's face it— could I, with that middle-class upbringing, have adapted myself to her environment? And yet this (in reverse) was just what I was expecting of Pam.

What have I been asking of her these past two years?

For quite a time now I have been a foster mother, and many people have asked me, 'Why did you do it?' mainly, I suppose, because I am single and it is unusual for a single woman to foster children. This has never been an easy question to answer, but it is one that I need to keep asking myself in order to keep a proper perspective and to save myself becoming bogged down in all the pettiness which can arise. My first, and easy, answer is to say that I have always wanted to do something like this. Even if I had married and had a family of my own I would not have felt justified in producing more children without trying to do something for those already in existence desperately in need of a home.

As a child during the war I lived in Wales, and there I

stayed very near a Children's Home and spent a great deal of time playing there. This obviously had some effect upon me. Since then I have had close contact with several other Homes—some large, some quite small. For a few months I worked in one as an assistant House Mother. In every case I felt that this was not the answer, although at the moment it seems to be the only system able to cope with the vast numbers. Living in an institution creates enormous problems in the lives of the children, apart from the very unnatural existence for the staff. The main difficulty for the children is that the staff are just staff. They are on duty and off duty. They have their own family and friends elsewhere and all this gives the children a feeling of imprisonment. There has not been one Home that I have visited where the children do not refer to the place as 'the prison'. On the other hand the staff are very cut off from their own people and the peculiar hours they work make it impossible for them to have a normal social life of their own, outside the Home. The actual organisation of these Homes is a very unenviable task. It is quite impossible to find enough of the right type of people to undertake such work—if they have the understanding then they don't have the physical strength or vice versa, and for this sort of child care to be successful it is essential to have both. There are a few, a very few people suited to this work and in these cases they do a grand job, but, from my experience, they are too few and far between and the children consequently suffer.

At the age of thirty-one I was unmarried and a shorthand-typist, and therefore fostering a child seemed to be quite out of the question so I did what I felt was the next best thing. I contacted a local Children's Home and offered to become an 'Auntie' to any child in need of extra attention, and in the months that followed I was introduced to Pam, a girl of twelve. I was told that she was a little backward, but that I would find out for myself to what extent, and from that point I plunged in, taking her out on Saturdays once a fortnight to start with.

It took a very long time, in fact many months, before I realised just how backward she was. These children are very

55

often aware and ashamed of their disabilities, and it was only as her confidence in me grew that she dared to admit her shortcomings. I realised ultimately that, at the age of twelve, she knew hardly anything at all. She couldn't read a word, couldn't tell the time, had no idea of the sequence of the months, the posting of letters, using a telephone, the existence of other countries and so on. In fact her whole life seemed to consist of eating, sleeping and fooling around—she did not even play as other children did.

At the age of thirteen Pam was sent to a school in London for educationally sub-normal children. During her three years there she did begin very simple reading, but her ability depended entirely upon her moods. At our Saturday meetings she would have one good day and about six dreadful ones when her mind appeared to be quite empty; but the fact that there was a slight sign of interest and effort once in a while encouraged me, and I, in turn, tried to encourage her. Unfortunately this school that she attended was in a terrible area and had many problems which she could well have done without, but there was nothing else for it at the time and so with the benefit of a little learning came the opportunity (if it can be called such) to mix with children in a position as bad if not worse than her own.

I increased her visits to me to every Saturday and took her away for several holidays, all of which helped to broaden her outlook. My family wrote letters to her and she, in turn, began to write (with a great deal of help) single-lined letters back and very, very slowly the tremendous gulf between 'existing' and 'living' was beginning to be bridged.

As the years passed I began to wonder just how she would manage when the time came for her to leave the Home. After all, that was only a temporary measure, and could provide shelter only until she was fifteen. In her case of extreme backwardness and need it might have been arranged for her to stay a year or two longer, but eventually she would have had to move on to a hostel in London. On one occasion, after an unfortunate incident with a man in a cinema when I had taken her to see an Elvis Presley film (the man turned out to be one of the porters she met on the railway station on the way to school) things did seem very desperate, so I took the bull by the horns and told the Superintendent of the Home where she was living that, if all the authorities thought fit, I would be prepared to make a home for her.

For me the next part of my life was one of the most tedious times through which I have ever had to live. I had made my offer and had to take a back seat while Housing Committees and Child Care Officers decided not only Pam's future, but mine too, because if the plan was to go ahead then it meant not only establishing a home (I had been living in a bed-sitter for three years) but also changing my employment so that I would have more suitable hours. After several months I heard that the Councils concerned had agreed to the plan so at least I was then in a position to start looking for new employment, which meant that at last I could really do something about it and start the preparations. But the long wait went on— I was waiting for a Council flat and although my name had been on the list for about seven years, I still had a further year to wait.

It is exceedingly difficult to uproot a fifteen-year-old (which is what Pam was by then). The news had to be broken to her very gently, and put as an invitation rather than a statement of fact. At first she was not at all sure that she wanted to come and live with me, which I suppose could have been disappointing, but I knew Pam and her fear of experiencing anything new. So far, I have said nothing of her past or family and the reasons for her being in the Home, but let this suffice for now to say that, because of all her wretched experiences in childhood, she had numbed her brain completely and she had refused to 'feel' life at all for many years and that what I was doing now was asking her to risk feeling again. With this daring to experience life came the very gradual progress, but with it also came the agonising understanding that she was different from other people.

The fostering relationship is a very queer one. One has all the work and responsibilities of a real mother, but that is as far as it goes. All children have a very strong basic need of their own parents, but fortunately children from normal homes do not have to keep thinking about this or proving it. These unhappy children, however, think and talk constantly about their families and a foster mother would be heading for much unhappiness if she ever imagined she took the place of the real mother, however much the real mother may have harmed her child, either through deliberate cruelty or total inadequacy to cope with motherhood—the latter being nearly always the case. A foster mother is faced constantly with situations which seem to be so unjust. The child often says, 'I'll tell my Mum of you—she never told me off like that', and so on, even though she hasn't seen her mother for years. It is at moments like this that I really have to hang on to my sanity and prevent myself from blurting out something I might greatly regret. In this particular case Pam's mother had abandoned seven children, and yet here was I being compared with her and criticised, when I was worn out and exasperated doing her job.

It was this new relationship with which I had to grapple in the first few months of our move into the flat. On the other hand the changes Pam had to face were tremendous, too. For about seven years she had lived a communal life, with at least fifteen children always in the same house, apart from several members of staff who were, as I have said, 'on duty and off duty'. To come and live with someone on her own was a wretched experience.

She did not move in all at once, but came for weekends to start with to get used to the feel of it. When eventually she did move in for good she used to follow me around saying, 'There ain't nuffink to do 'ere.' That was not really true, of course, as one of the first things I did before she moved in was to arrange for there to be all sorts of things for her to do, including some she had started before even I had moved into the flat, so that everything wouldn't be completely strange; but she must have felt so lost that she couldn't bring herself to settle to anything. In the end I had to get really cross with her and *order* her to do a specific task.

To be a House Mother in a Home, with probably fifteen children to control, is no easy task and, as I said at the beginning, it is very rare indeed to be able to find someone who can control that number in a proper manner—you need to be fully trained and experienced in order to do this. If a House Mother has only a very small knowledge of psychology, and is exhausted as well—as she very likely will be—then the only way to get control is to shout or even resort to physical punishment.

Pam had been brought up in this way in recent years and she, therefore, responded to very little else. For a long time I tried every other way I knew, coaxing, reasoning, even small bribes, but in the end I had to resort to shouting. I felt very ashamed of myself, felt as though I had failed, but to my astonishment it worked, and after a few tears she improved no end. I changed my tactics accordingly and became a domineering brute! In that state of mind she was really only happy and secure when she was taking orders. As far as I dared I encouraged her to take decisions for herself, both about clothes, and doing small jobs at home, but it didn't work for very long. One example was her own bed-making. She knew very well how to do it as this is a job they do for themselves in Homes from a very early age. I decided to check it once in a while to make sure that it was all right and to my horror I found that she was sleeping with the bed in chaos. I came to the conclusion that she was prepared to suffer anything in order to feel discipline exerted, and this has proved to be the case on many occasions since.

From then on I found my new role very exacting. It was a question of giving commands, and then making quite sure that they were carried out. I had to think carefully before I made threats as I knew they would have to be fulfilled once uttered. It is very easy to threaten, hoping that the threat itself will be enough incentive, but in this case she was testing me all the time to see how much I could take, and whether I really meant what I said. The thing I found most difficult was the pettiness of the testing. It was nearly always over wretchedly small things which hardly seemed worth all the fights we had. Nevertheless, I knew I couldn't back down as this would have shown the weakness she was looking for and dreading. It was a question of dirty finger nails, lack of shoe cleaning, careless washing-up, careless ironing, untidy hair, scruffy clothes and so on. She has even been known to wear a thick winter coat in the middle of a heat-wave in June, just so that she could feel me exert discipline. It wasn't that she *couldn't* cope for herself. She quite deliberately did things wrongly, hoping that I would notice and nag. I would never have believed a child could want to live like this, especially when she had the chance of plenty of attention and a happy, friendly atmosphere for the first time in her life. But she couldn't—it was strange to her, and so she forced me to become a tyrant just because that sort of treatment was familiar and the only feeling of stability she had.

One of the things she had to conquer on moving in with me was her fear of sleeping alone. When living at home with her family, six of the children had shared a bedroom, the four girls, Jean, Pam, Alice and Julie sleeping in one bed (Julie was only two years old then) and two of the boys, Jim, the eldest and coloured, and Johnny in another bed. Ronnie, the baby, was sleeping in the same room as Mum and Dad. (When the family split up a few months later, Ronnie, who was not at all strong, was fostered by a young couple who already had two boys of their own, and so lost contact with the rest of his own family. He was too young to remember them. However, the others did not forget him and they missed him so much. To them he was always their 'baby' who had been taken away. The situation became more difficult and eventually it was decided that it would be as well if one of the others could see him and be able to tell the others that he was well and happy. Jean was chosen, but she had to promise her Child Care Officer that she would not tell Ronnie who she really was when she did meet him. This she did do, although it must have been very hard for her. The main thing was that she had seen him and found him to be a normal, happy boy surrounded by a family who cared for him and this news she was able to pass on to the others, which did allay their fears a little. No doubt a day will come when Ronnie does have to find out about the rest of his real family, but it will not be easy to find the right time to tell him—he is bound to be hurt and shocked by the news.)

To revert to Pam. In the Home she had been in small dormitories and there was a constant coming and going. Now, for the first time in her life she was to sleep in a room on her own. I had foreseen difficulties ahead over this and had bought some night-lights; I had also left both our bedroom doors open. It was a long time before she slept without a dread of someone climbing up the drainpipe and in through her bedroom window! She used to shout out in her sleep, waking me on many occasions, and the language she used was quite fantastic! I had never heard such words spoken before. The strange thing was that she never swore in front of me during her waking hours. She must have controlled her tongue at home as it became very evident that this was her everyday language at school.

Another trial to her in the early days was my insistence on the use of handkerchiefs. When I had taken her away for weekends previously she had been supplied with a few new ones but to have a clean one every day was apparently not the custom at the Home. I had always kept paper ones ready when she used to visit me, just in case she needed one, but now it was a question of training her to use them regularly—not an easy habit to form when you are fifteen; the more natural methods are far more simple!

She looked upon me and mine as 'posh' and it was this 'poshness' she fought in every respect, over speech, social behaviour, table manners and so on. She had obviously had no real training at the right time anyway and this inverted snobbery made the task even harder. The way she sat at table and held cutlery was appalling; the way she chewed with her mouth open—everything. I knew that if she was to be accepted normally in the area in which we lived, all this would have to be changed. I also knew that I couldn't change everything at once as it would make life unbearable for both of us, so I started the belated training checking one fault at a time. It took weeks of persistent nagging on one aspect alone, and just as she seemed to be accepting one correction I started on another. We went on like this for months and months, until there was a gradual, general improvement, and then I eased off the nagging. Even this I couldn't stop abruptly as she missed it and immediately gave me cause to start again. She had no idea how to hold food in her hands and would sit eating, say, bread, butter and jam with her fingers right in the middle of the slice and get covered with jam. She seemed totally unaware of the stickiness and when she had left the table I would find door handles, paintwork and so on daubed with jam. This also applied to eating fruit. I formed the routine of going round behind her after she had eaten to wipe everything with a damp cloth.

When she came to me she was already attending the school for educationally sub-normal in London. It meant a train journey every day and she seemed to cope with this fairly well. She didn't travel alone as she was joined by one or two others from the same school who were still living at the Home. She was usually home on time, but very often her clothes were in a shocking state; for example, on one occasion her raincoat was chalked all over by some of the boys. This had happened on the way to the railway station in London. There was nothing I could do about it, and in many ways I was thankful I wasn't there to see what was going on. I know there were 'flirtations' with some of the porters on the station, and the rough play that went on in the streets would have driven me to distraction if I had seen it. Months after she had left school I found one of her school blouses scribbled all over with the words RINGO STARR in ink. It had to be thrown away.

When she came to live with me I had to give her a front door key of her own. I knew it was a risk, but I had to take it as she was home from school a little before I came home from work and I didn't want her roaming the streets until I arrived. As a rule she was always home at least half an hour before me so, when one day about six weeks after her arrival, I found her not at home on my return from work, I had quite a shock. At first I put it down to the trains being late. I prepared the meal, becoming more and more anxious as I did so. I waited for a little while, looking out of the window and listening for her steps on the stairs, but still there was no sign of her. I decided to try and eat something myself, thinking that if I was going to have to go out in search of her, I had better not start out hungry. By this time it was about 7 o'clock and quite dark outside. I was feeling thoroughly weak as I felt sure by now that she had run away and I couldn't think what had gone so wrong, particularly at that time, as there was no obvious reason just then. (There have been many times since when I would have believed it possible!) I had already searched her bedroom to see what coat she was wearing and if she had taken anything special with her, and had been horrified to find that she had taken a framed photograph of her House Mother from the Home. This was enough to convince me that she really had run away.

I decided to telephone the Superintendent of the Home to ask his advice, and just as I got through to him I saw a shadow move close to the shop windows. I asked him to wait while I had a look, and sure enough, there she was, walking along, crying, thoroughly miserable and hungry. I told the Superintendent that she was found and then took her home and fed her first— she had had nothing since dinner time—and gradually the story unfolded. She had had no thoughts of running away. She and her friends had been fooling around outside the railway station and she had put her satchel down by a pillar box while she chased another girl; when she got back it had disappeared. She must have spent several hours wandering around looking for it, and had finally decided to catch a train home, having first gone to the police (quite an achievement, I thought) but she was too scared to come indoors, mainly because the front door key was lost with the satchel and she was terrified of the consequences. Needless to say I had dinned in the importance and value of the key when I had given it to her. I felt quite sure that she had suffered enough so I went with her to the local railway station to report the loss. I think she now realised that I didn't get furious over genuine accidents and also that I was prepared to 'move heaven and earth' for

63

her in order to put things right. I, in turn, learned not to jump to conclusions. She had had no thoughts of running away and I had been in a near panic quite unnecessarily.

It was a fortnight before I had a postcard from Waterloo Station saying that the satchel had been found and was awaiting collection. As she was already at school in the London area I decided to take the plunge and let her go to Waterloo herself. She did manage it quite all right, and I think felt a great deal better for having put things right on her own. I am thankful to say that the contents of the satchel had been untouched, and so I did not need to go to the trouble of changing the lock on the front door. I am now always optimistic about a certain amount of good coming from every 'tragedy'!

I was very thankful when an opportunity came for me to get her away from school. It was obvious that she was not likely to learn much more there, and the company she was keeping was doing very much more harm than good.

During this first six months I had come to realise just what I was up against. However, we were already beginning to break the back of the enormous task, and despite the uphill work and many trials and tribulations on both sides, slight improvements were beginning to show and I felt encouraged to struggle on.

Pam left school at last. I had already found her a job and this was being kept open until she was free to leave school. Of course, she could not do anything that involved reading or writing so it was arranged that she should start by washing up in the kitchens of a local rehabilitation centre.

I tried to prepare her for this change in status and to install a sense of responsibility into her, but her first few weeks were terrible. She hardly worked at all and if it had not been for one of her colleagues covering up for her, she might not be there now. I might add that this colleague was, herself, confined to a wheelchair. It was not until some weeks after she had been 'working' that I discovered that she was not eating at all in the middle of the day. I suppose she was too embarrassed to eat in front of other people—a very natural feeling, but most youngsters manage to face up to it. This meant that by the middle of the afternoon she was more or less unable to cope with work through hunger. Once again her colleagues came to the rescue and in time coaxed her to eat normally with the rest. Her work was still not good and in the end I had to get really cross with her and point out that it would mean the 'sack' if she did not pull her weight properly. I was very fortunate in having this colleague Elizabeth to back me up. Although handicapped, she had been doing her own work and Pam's which was hardly a fair way of going on, and I was able to shame Pam into action at last.

As always, 'birds of a feather flock together', and unfortunately for Pam, she was no exception. Because of her own disabilities she had to seek employment of the most simple kind, and naturally she soon found that many of her colleagues were in the same position as herself for one reason or another. Because of their small-mindedness she had to live in a very unhappy atmosphere in some respects, and there was a great deal of petty unpleasantness and jealousy. It was a very great blessing that there were some people on her side and they counteracted the sharp attacks from the others. Pam too, had very little control over her tongue and if she were hurt then she would hit back, verbally or literally. I think that on the occasions when she was most spiteful to me at home it was after some upset at work, and I was the only person she dared to hit back at to any extent.

Despite these unfortunate relationships, she was extremely lucky in others. Elizabeth I have already mentioned. She was handicapped herself and married to a handicapped man, but she had one of the most serene faces I have ever seen and she seemed to 'mother' Pam in a remarkable way. Maybe the friendship with Pam helped Elizabeth, too, as she would never have any children of her own, but whatever the reasons, she did wonders with her. I shall never forget visiting her home. Everything was designed for people living in wheelchairs, but nevertheless the whole flat was kept beautifully. I always feel very ashamed of my own efforts in this direction when I think of her.

The people that really mattered at work, namely the Matron, her secretary and the occupational therapists, only tolerated Pam to start with, but gradually they seemed to begin to like her quite genuinely and they steered her through many difficult times. Pam was always 'good for a laugh' at work and I think she probably brightened the place quite a bit, if she didn't actually earn her living washing up!

Her greatest failing had always been 'men' and on the surface it looked very bad. I pointed out to Matron right from the start that she did tend to turn to men for company rather than women and that the main reason was that the father of the family had remained very loyal, the mother having been the one to let them down completely. Matron seemed to understand, though she often said that men were Pam's downfall! It was especially difficult with the patients, who were, themselves, very much deprived of normal relationships with the opposite sex and I am afraid Pam had several hard lessons to learn in this direction, but more of that later.

Ever since she had lived with me she had played with dolls, but the intensity of her playing depended on how she was feeling emotionally. Although she had a much larger vocabulary by this time, she never attempted to express her feelings in words and, therefore, the dolls were the only method I had of knowing that anything was wrong. If ever she was unsettled the dolls came to life again and when she was feeling happier they could drift into insignificance. It was only when Julie eventually came to live with us the following June that Pam decided quite firmly that she would have no more to do with dolls because she was afraid Julie would laugh at her.

I mentioned earlier the deep need these children have for their own parents, whatever the circumstances. Pam had seen her father regularly as he had visited the Home every Sunday from the beginning, and I had encouraged her to join the others when he came. It meant going to the Home each time and this was not very successful, partly through Pam's own fault and partly through the lack of understanding shown by her

House Parents. I persuaded her to keep up the visits, though, for the sake of the father who had been so loyal for so long. This, however, was not enough for her. It became more and more apparent that she was thinking of her mother, who had abandoned them all. She half hated her and half wanted her and these emotions were tearing her apart. In the end I asked her if she would really like to meet her mother if she had the chance, and she said she would.

I contacted the Child Care Officer and she said that, if I was prepared to risk it, then we could make the necessary arrangements, but we both felt it would be much better for Pam to have this first meeting with her mother at our home rather than Pam go to the mother's which she had never seen before as the mother had since moved in with another man. The arrangements for the visit were finally made and Jean, the older sister who had been in touch with the mother since she had left the Home, was going to bring her down from London to see us.

It was a very tense time for all of us. I was so thankful for a beautiful sunny day, which I am sure must have helped. Pam had not seen her mother for many years and was, therefore, full of apprehension. She was convinced her mother would not come and all the morning she kept saying how she hated her. I endeavoured to keep as calm an atmosphere as possible, but it was not easy. I, myself, was keyed right up, wondering what on earth such a woman was going to be like. I arranged to be out when she arrived, thinking that it would be quite an emotional meeting, but unfortunately the mother was a little later than expected and I just got home in time to see Jean walking along the road with this woman, so I went in and called to Pam that she was here. To my astonishment Pam stopped for nothing and flew down the stairs, along the road and into her mother's arms. Once indoors she was very tearful for about half an hour, so I kept out of the way again, but after that everything went very smoothly. The mother seemed a nice enough woman to talk to, and behaved reasonably throughout. She couldn't take her eyes off Pam whom she had not seen since she was a little girl of nine. Apart from that it was a most ordinary visit. We showed her photographs of her other children that I had taken during the past four years. I felt most odd doing this—almost embarrassed, in fact, not to mention an 'intruder'. She, however, showed no signs of emotion. She was very interested, but that was all. After that we played gramophone records and at about 7 o'clock she got ready to leave. While she was indoors she had said nothing about the past, but once on the doorstep, where anyone could have overheard, she made endless excuses for her behaviour and condemned her husband. She made promises to write to Pam every Saturday, sending her 5/- a week, but not one letter has been received from that day to this, despite the fact that Pam has written to her on several occasions.

I felt quite exhausted after she had gone, mainly I think, because everything had gone so smoothly; I had been expecting the worst and when she came she couldn't have been more ordinary. This episode, of course, gave the whole picture of the family break-up. The mother, though full of good intentions, was totally inadequate and unable to bring herself to take any action regarding her children.

This meeting with her mother gave Pam a very new outlook on her own situation. Children 'in care' always tend to think that 'they' (the Child Care Officers) have taken them away from their parents and that the parents are quite innocent. In the Home Pam had been taught to hate her mother by one member of staff, but I had always felt that this active hating of someone she had not seen for years was doing her no good. On the other hand, she had to know that it was the mother who had let them down, whatever the reason. This visit to us, and the subsequent further lack of attention from the mother after all the promises, brought home to Pam the real truth, and very painful it was. In fact, she had to realise that her mother, whilst being quite ordinary and likeable, had not got enough 'go' in her even to write letters or send birthday cards to her children.

Needless to say the dolls were very much in evidence for the few weeks following, especially when she was watching the postman, looking for the promised letter which never came.

But having been rejected in the past, she was very quick to accept the situation a second time and she gave up hope within two or three weeks. Poor Pam!

Dad was a pathetic little man, partially crippled. He did, however, do all that he could for his children, and this was more than most of these parents did. He was exceptionally loyal, struggling down Sunday after Sunday. I am quite sure this loyalty made an enormous difference in the lives of his children—it was the one real anchor they had. I don't know that his motives were one hundred per cent on the side of the children—he was terribly lonely, and these Sunday visits were probably the highlight of his life. He also stayed at the Home during Christmas and always came to us on Boxing Day with the rest of his family from the Home. He came to tea with us once a month as well. I don't know what to say about these visits. I know the children were glad to have him in their home, and sometimes I deliberately left them alone together so that he could feel himself to be the head of his family, without interference, but I don't think he really assumed his position. He just sat in an armchair and talked and the conversation was not particularly inspiring. He tried to 'guide' his children, but his approach was so hopeless. However, I am sure his loyalty outshone his inadequacy in this respect.

This was the man that Pam had looked upon as her father. He had married his wife when she already had two illegitimate children, Jim the coloured boy, and Jean, and he treated these two just as his own. At one of my early meetings with him he asked me if I would like to see a photograph of his eldest son, and naturally I said I would. I hope the shock I felt didn't register on my face when I was presented with this photograph of an enormous coloured boy! He really did treat him as if he were his own. On marrying his wife, five more children were added to his family, the eldest being Pam. Her attitude towards him was odd, on looking back, although in the early stages I put it down to her general backwardness. Sometimes she wanted to see him, and sometimes she didn't, and I often had

69

to encourage her to go and meet him on Sundays. Then, one day, from a source right outside the Home, I heard a rumour that he wasn't Pam's father. I immediately realised that if this were true, it could account for all her peculiar attitudes towards him. I mentioned the possibility to the Child Care Officer and a tactful questioning was made from that end. Dad finally admitted that it was true. He had married the mother, and then found that she was expecting a third illegitimate child. The secret had been kept for fifteen years but, after much discussion, we decided that Pam had obviously had it in her mind for quite some time and that, although it would be a great shock to her initially, truth would be better than doubt. It was arranged that I should be the one to tell her at the first opportunity. I took the plunge as soon as possible. It was a complete realisation of all her fears and her reaction was immediate tears which didn't subside for some time. I put it to her that she was like her sister, Jean, and therefore they would be very close now. I suggested she should write to her at once (the idea being to give her something concrete to do about it) and this she did. From then on her main worry was wondering whether she would be rejected by the other brothers and sisters, as she wasn't really one of them, although she legally bore their name as she was born after the mother had married Dad. This was a terrible burden for a backward girl especially at the age of fifteen—why she couldn't have known all along like the other two I don't know. However, once the secret was out and she had discussed the matter openly with Dad she, and he I might add, felt a great deal happier about it and I think they have since built up a much better relationship. At least she could see that he never rejected her, and he treated her as his own, by the fact that he himself had kept the secret, and not even told the Child Care Officer.

Having accepted the fact that her Dad was not her real father, and then having met her mother for the first time in years, at Pam's request visits to their respective homes were arranged. I was not all that happy about it as I knew that in both cases

70

the conditions wouldn't be good, but she had a right to know, and if she wanted to see for herself, then it wasn't for me to stop her.

She had looked forward so much to seeing her mother's home. Jean had agreed to meet her at Victoria Station so that they could travel together to the mother's rooms, for that was all she had. Here Pam was introduced to 'Uncle Charlie', Mum's boyfriend. Mum had lived with him for the past seven years. Although Pam had obviously enjoyed her day with her own family, on arriving home she was torn between the two 'worlds' with which she was confronted. The day was spoilt by the sense of shame she felt for the way in which her own family lived. Apparently Uncle Charlie, from her description, was little more than an animal, and several times Jean had to ask Mum to tell him to keep his hands off her. Pam was particularly shocked at this as she had recently been told that Jean was expecting her first child (illegitimate)—yet another shock for Pam—and for Uncle Charlie to keep on pestering Jean when she was in that condition was too disgusting! Whether Mum succeeded in stopping her boyfriend 'making love' to her daughter I don't know. I rather doubt it!

From then on Pam began to see very clearly the different ways of life, the one which was hers by birth, and the new way which I was trying to teach her—the way she had always thought of as 'posh' but which she was now beginning to see was the usual and accepted standard with 'normal' families. She often used to say to me, 'I don't never want to be like Jean', meaning, of course, she didn't want to have an illegitimate child, with no husband and no decent home of her own. Her aims began to be very high, but her leanings towards men were just as strong as ever, and the only reason that she was not in the same position as Jean was that I was still able to steer her into company where the men she did meet did not take advantage of her weakness. I tried hard to make her understand that all men and all women were very strongly attracted to each other, but that if we wanted decent homes for ourselves and our children, we must all strive to control our natural feelings.

71

As she already felt so different from other people it was essential that I made her understand that her feelings in this direction were perfectly normal; it was just that all men and women must learn to control themselves.

While she was with her mother she had the opportunity to ask about her real father. This was not very satisfactory. All the mother told her was that Jimmy, the coloured boy, had one father, Jean had another who was killed in the war, and that Pam herself had another father, but who he was or anything about him she wouldn't say—so Pam was left high and dry. She brought home a paper-bag full of small things from her mother, including old photographs of the family taken while they still lived together, and these in some small way compensated for the let-downs of the day.

I have always felt that the only way to steer her through these very trying experiences was to open all doors and let her see and decide for herself which was the way of life she would choose to follow (although I must admit that I have, at times, wanted to cut her off from the past that was hurting her so much). Had I shut her off from her family and all that it meant, I am convinced she would have fought me in order to contact them again, and under those circumstances she would undoubtedly have chosen their way of life. As it was, I gave her complete freedom to visit both sides of her family as and when she wanted to, and so she was able to form her own judgments. Quite frequently she talked to me about her family, and it was at these times that I was able to express my own opinions and also put both sides of the story clearly. Naturally she heard very biased opinions from both parents.

Before long, she asked if she could go and see Dad in his home. Once again she was very excited at the prospect, and went to quite unusual trouble over her appearance. She was to make this journey alone, but as she had been to school in the area, it was not too difficult and Dad would be at the station to meet her. He was, himself, quite a decent little man and her relationship with him had become much more sound now that the truth was out in the open and they could talk about it together.

Unfortunately his surroundings were not good. He had taken in his wife's sister, her husband and three children into his small flat, against the landlord's instructions, and they were not ideal neighbours. Apparently there was a row between them and another family a floor above which ended in a fight while Pam was there. Dad had to lend money to Pam's uncle in order to stop the fight. Pam came home disgusted. The fight was the worst thing, but even the children were badly cared for, in her opinion.

During the afternoon the uncle and all his family went out in the car—they could afford to run a car—taking Pam and Dad with them. I had asked Pam to try and get home as near 8.30 as possible as I visualised her travelling alone. She had always been very good about keeping to time and when 9 o'clock arrived I began to be really worried. At 9.30 I went to the station to meet the train but she was not on it. I repeated this every half hour until I had seen the 10.30 train in, by which time I was frantic. I went back to the flat for my scooter keys as I decided the only way to find out if she had left Dad's home was to ask the local police to make contact through the police near his home. I wondered if he had decided to put her up for the night, which would most certainly have been the lesser of many evils. I visualised her on a wrong train, completely lost—or even worse! Just as I was at my most desperate I heard a car door bang. I flew down the concrete stairs yet again, to see her being brought in by a man I did not know. He turned out to be her uncle. They had continued their drive and were on their way home then—10.45 by this time. I can't remember what I said, but I am sure I wasn't all that gracious. These sort of people seem quite unable to put themselves into anyone else's place. As I said to Dad the following weekend, he would have been very angry with me had there really been something wrong and I had taken no action. I think he understood how I felt then and we parted friends. Poor Pam, having had a very full and disturbing day anyway, came home to find me in this frantic state. But still, at least she saw that I was ready to take action on her behalf, even to the extent of going to the police—unheard of in her family. Police are enemies in their eyes: so perhaps a few lessons were learned, but with the useful lessons came yet another shaming experience.

At this stage she had one further outing with her family which caused us an upset. This time the uncle and family called at the Home one Sunday afternoon to take them all out on a surprise trip to the coast. She arrived home in very reasonable time, but unfortunately I looked out of the window just in time to see her walking along our road eating a dreadful 'rock dummy' sweet and wearing one of those awful seaside hats. She came in thrilled with her afternoon and I blame myself entirely for all that followed, although I shall always feel the same about the hat! Whenever I have passed a crowd of people wearing 'kiss-me-quick' hats at the seaside I have always felt embarrassed for them. I wish I could have felt a little less strongly, but my disapproval at seeing her walking along the road wearing the hat and sucking the 'dummy' must have shown all over my face and she knew immediately, once again, the enormous gulf between us. I did not destroy the hat, but said she could keep it for playing indoors, and that it was not to be worn outside. She expressed her feelings by trying to go out in it the following day when she thought I wasn't looking, but I caught her!

I think perhaps my single status comes to the fore over this sort of thing. I am terrified that she might attract the wrong type and, being alone at home, I would find it impossible to cope if she started to have 'undesirable callers'.

So far, she had only been living with me for about eight months, and in this short time she had been very rudely awakened to what life was about and her own situation in relation to others; but the secrets that had been torturing her mind all her life were out now. All that had hurt her so much had been put right (as far as this was possible). It was rather like the completion of a major operation and now all she had to do was to get well. She would always bear the scars, but the wounds would heal.

As with any physical surgery, quite a large part of the 'after care' is treatment for shock. Pam had received more shocks in these last few months than one would expect anyone to have to bear in a lifetime. Let me list them to give some idea of the impact on her very limited brain.

(1) The knowledge that she had a very limited brain and had not been able to be educated as others. This she had realised.

(2) The confirmation that 'Dad' was not her real father, and with it the realisation of her actual relationship to her brothers and sisters and strong fear that they would reject her if they found out.

(3) The fact that Mum was the one who had broken the family, and that she had no inclination to do anything for her family even now.

(4) The way in which both sides of her family lived were contrary to the accepted standards of 'normal' people.

(5) That Jean, her sister, only one year older than herself, was expecting an illegitimate baby, the father of whom was coloured.

Having already said so much about the difficulties she experienced on moving in with me, and then starting work, I have not listed them here, but the 'surgery' she had gone through in this short time was terrible.

We settled down into a fairly steady and fast routine—fast mainly because it gave her less time to think and brood (apart from the fact that we both had to be out of the flat soon after eight o'clock in the mornings and then I taught at evening classes and she had her week-night routine) and for a time things went quite well. Most of the time she looked very slovenly—she walked badly and was clumsy in all movements, to the extent that I wondered if there was brain damage causing both the backwardness and the lack of co-ordination.

Her right eye had always bothered me, ever since I had been introduced to her. It didn't 'pull' with the other one. I had noticed that it was worse if she was under any sort of stress, for example meeting new people and so on, but, of course, there was nothing I could do while she was living in the Home. Now came my opportunity. I took her to my optician and my doubts were confirmed. Although there was not anything actually wrong with the eye, she hadn't used it for years and it was consequently out of action. No wonder she had found reading difficult, and this may have been one of the initial causes of her backwardness. Her attitude towards anyone in authority was one of fear, and it was extremely difficult for the optician to make a thorough test. For one thing, I had had to warn him that she couldn't read much (possibly 'and' and 'it' and a few little words like that) and also the darkened room and all the gadgets terrified her. She sat in the chair, clutching my hand, while I translated all the optician said. Her vocabulary was so small that my role as interpreter was really essential! He tested her eyes as 'painlessly' as possible and decided to give her some glasses. Her reaction on hearing that she would have to wear glasses was a little violent, so he advised me not to press the matter too strongly but to try and get her to wear them for watching television, sewing, and any other close work. After several months of little ups and downs in this direction she did accept them fairly well, until the day she had to have her eyes re-tested. This was brought about by continual aching and watering of the offending eye. When she was told she had to wear them all the time there was a minor revolution! The optician drew me aside and said that, although she definitely needed glasses all the time now, it looked as though the emotional upsets would far outweigh the lack of sight and discomfort, and that under no circumstances was I to force the issue. Since then she has refused to wear them, even for close work, so we are now right back where we started. What a tragedy that this wasn't noticed and dealt with when she was still young enough to benefit from treatment. If her mother had been a normal woman, this would probably have been rectified at a very early age.

Although the outcome of this episode was not as intended, at least she had had one new experience and something new to think about (an all-important factor in getting her brain to function again), so perhaps it wasn't completely wasted.

Another ordeal in this direction was her annual visit to my doctor, this being a condition of the fostering. From her behaviour on these occasions I dread to think of the treatment she must have had in the past—or is it just that all children 'in care' put up a fight at every opportunity? Fortunately my doctor had a real 'way' with children and her experience here was not as terrifying as it might have been, in fact it was a rather humorous encounter. He soon put her at her ease, and in this state she can be very funny—all the Cockney in her coming to the fore. At one point he asked her for a 'specimen' and she gave me an enquiring look so I said, 'Just go with the lady [his nurse] and spend a penny as she tells you'. Pam laughed and said, 'Oh, now I know wot yer mean!' I don't think the doctor had ever had such a patient, but the whole affair turned out to be much more light-hearted than she imagined and she began to like him and have faith in him, which was an excellent step forward.

Last but not least came a visit to the dentist. This was beyond my worst nightmares! I had foreseen difficulties, and told her that if she stuck it out well, then there would be a little reward. I had to go in with her. I had previously warned the dentist that she was backward so he was partially prepared. She got into the chair quite well and he made his preliminary inspection. His great mistake was in announcing the fact that six fillings would be necessary! From her high perch she began to climb out of the chair crying, 'No, no—I won't 'ave it.' I gave one short, sharp command to stay just where she was. The panic-stricken dentist called me into a little side room to discuss the matter. He felt that if he didn't do something easy that day, he would never be able to get near her, and I quite agreed. He started to do the smallest filling—giving an injection first. When she saw the needle she began to cry out again—long before it reached her mouth, and when the injection began to take she went completely to pieces, being quite unprepared for the sensation of numbness. It was quite a struggle—two of us held her down while the dentist used all the skill he knew. He really was marvellous with her and eventually the mission was completed. She made more appointments for the other five fillings, and with much persuasion (and bribery) I managed to get her to agree to face it alone next time. I had the feeling that she would get a better grip on herself without me. I don't know who was most scared when the time arrived for treatment, Pam or the dentist; but it worked—she behaved herself and he was amazed. It is at times like these that I panic too, as, under very great stress, she is liable to forget herself and those naughty little words are likely to come tumbling out. I have had no ill reports since, so I can only assume one of two things; either she controlled herself, or he wasn't shocked!

In the early days time had seemed to drag in some ways. I used to think, 'She's been with me a whole month; I wonder how things will be this time next month', and so on. But in time, once the routine was established, time began to drift by and after some of the early upheavals already mentioned, we came to a much more settled and happy period. In the block of flats where we lived Pam was beginning to be known for herself and not as 'one of the kids from the Home'. (We lived a little too near the Home in some respects.)

Every Monday evening Pam visited a friend of mine with a young family, and there she was caught up in the small domesticities of ordinary family life. She formed a great many of her early opinions on how a home should be run in this environment and frequently made such comments as, 'Auntie always has Uncle's dinner ready on the table when he comes home from work.' All this was new to her, and it was such a blessing that I had a friend who was prepared to accept her just as she was and let her mix with her own young children—who knows what language they picked up—a Cockney accent would have been the least of her worries!

On Wednesdays she went to Cubs as a 'helper'. Again she was more than fortunate in the Leaders in charge of her. They were so very understanding. Their idea was to teach her something quite simple in advance, like skipping, knots, or even first-aid later on—something practical anyway—and then let her teach the boys. Slowly but surely she found she was able to impart knowledge to others and this was a great boost to her ego. She also listened with the boys to the stories that were told. This was a wonderful opportunity to catch up on a lost childhood. Eventually she gained enough confidence to keep the score for their team games. I think one of the greatest triumphs at that time was when they gave her a Cub Leader's uniform and she actually started to wear it. She had never worn a uniform in her life and it was good to see her beginning to conform. The hat was a bit of a problem, but I have seen her in it! I should add that, although she was wearing the uniform, she always wore a big coat over it, even in the hall, whatever the weather, but one step at a time—improvement is improvement after all. Things were not always straightforward at Cubs. Although I said she never swore in front of me at home, I am afraid she used this as a way of finding out just how much people outside would take from her, testing them to see if they would reject her, as she had been so many times before. This swearing did cause some trouble, quite understandably, but the offended parents were ultimately calmed and she was allowed to stay on. Although I realised the seriousness of this sort of thing (for it was no ordinary swearing, in fact the minister classified it as obscene!) I did feel that so many people had their priorities wrong. They didn't trouble to find out why she was doing it, and were quite ready to have her thrown out. If I know anything about Cubs, they probably knew all the words she was likely to use anyway, and the damage she could do them *in comparison* with the damage that would be done to her if she had been rejected, would have been negligible. After all, they all came from good homes; but I know now that many people from 'good' homes set such a high standard for themselves and those around them that they are quite out of touch with the lives of people like Pam and her family, and they just cannot make the necessary allowances. I was really furious over this and was quite ready to see if it could be arranged for us to move into London where this sort of thing wouldn't matter so much. However, it didn't have to come to that, but it left me feeling very bitter.

We jogged along quite happily after that for several months, and she really did begin to improve quite a lot, although, of course, such improvement was slow in comparison with others of her age. I took her to my parents for a weekend, and here she surprised them in the poise she was beginning to develop. She seemed to hold her head better, walk better and there was occasionally an element of charm in her manner.

The Child Care Officer visited us and had long talks with Pam on her own, and every now and again I would go up to London to see her where we discussed the whole family situation as well as Pam's own particular problems. It was at one of these meetings that I was asked if I would consider taking another child. From the very beginning I had always said that I would be prepared to if it was thought advisable because I was so very aware of the loneliness Pam would have to suffer, living alone with me after having had so many around her.

This time I had my own ideas on who I would like to join us. Naturally it would be one of the family. There were three of them left in the Home: Alice, aged fourteen; Johnnie, aged twelve (he was out of the question as I had no spare bedroom for a boy, and in any case he needed a man); and Julie, aged ten. I had had more to do with Alice than the others in the past as she had been on holiday with us, but I felt that if I had her, she and Pam were too close in age, especially in view of Pam's backwardness, and there would be constant friction. They would also probably 'gang up' on me and I might not be able to control them together. There were so many pros and cons, but I eventually decided that if I was going to have another one at all, it would have to be Julie, first because she and Pam were very much closer than Pam and Alice (Pam always loved the younger ones, probably because she felt she could keep one step ahead of them) and, second, because I felt that if I took Julie at the age of ten I could do more for her starting so much younger. I hated making the decision. As far as Pam had been concerned, I had deliberately made no choice at all, feeling that normal parents have to accept what comes and that that would be a far better start to the relationship, and I think I was right. However, despite the pain I know I caused Alice by passing her by, I am sure I did make the right choice in Julie, and in any case the Child Care Officers agreed with my decision, too, so it eased my conscience a little.

Having made the decision I had to arrange the announcement of this great news to Pam so that it would look as though she had done the choosing! There had been times when I was very thankful for her backwardness, although she could be quite shrewd at times. This time, however, I managed to steer her choice to Julie, and for a week or so she was very excited about the whole idea. Of course, it had to be kept a very close secret until the 'right' moment came for breaking the news to the rest of the family. As for Pam, so Alice and Johnnie had to feel that they were taking the decision as to which of them should come to me. This was handled in a most ingenious manner and although there was a little upset at the time of the move, they all felt that they had taken the decision, and that it was in the hands of their family, and not the Authorities.

After this, our peaceful time was over. Pam became quite difficult again, playing up as she had done when she first came, and becoming very babyish. All the improvements disappeared. I could hardly believe it as she had been so thrilled at the idea at first.

About this time she started to receive letters from an 'old boyfriend', an Irish lad of seventeen. This meant she, too, had to write some letters! I drafted them for her as, of course, she still couldn't express herself at all in writing. She didn't seem at all embarrassed at showing me his letters or asking me to write for her. How terrible it is to be so dependent upon someone. He kept asking her to meet him so I decided the best thing would be for him to visit us at home. We arranged a Saturday afternoon. Saturday mornings at home were always chaos because, with me working full time during the week, everything had to be done on a Saturday, including washing, shopping and housework. We had rushed through the chores and were just sitting down to a hasty salad lunch so that she would be ready for him, when there was a knock at the door, and there he stood. Pam hadn't seen him for over a year and her reaction must have been very off-putting. She took one look at him, turned to me muttering, 'he's changed', and disappeared into the kitchen. Needless to say she was still wearing all her working clothes of the morning and looked frightful. What a meeting! She eventually managed to go into the sitting room and speak to him. He, too, had been at an E.S.N. school, but I don't think he could have been as bad as Pam. I managed to share our salad between three instead of two—not much of a dinner for a boy. This wonderful romance lasted three weeks, I am thankful to say, although the aftermath was worse than if it had never happened. Once again she had been rejected.

She began to make her life, and mine, a misery. She was as unhappy as she had ever been and as disobedient, too. She seemed to be looking for things to annoy me. This meant that, instead of giving her the understanding she needed so much (and I was the only person who knew the whole story), she was forcing me to be cross with her every moment of her waking hours. I began to dread waking up, and was thankful I had a job to go to. Pam took refuge in her bicycle. We had a double line of garages where we lived and she used to cycle round and round between them for hours at a time. I just had to let her go. If I tried to talk to her it made more trouble. I suppose, on looking back, that I was the one person in the world that she dared to be horrid to and I was consequently taking the hurts that she would have liked to have inflicted on all the people who hurt her. The only person that could help was our next door neighbour. He used to just listen to her tales of woe. Often he found her crying alone on our balcony, and then she would pour out all her troubles to him. She began to talk quite frequently of suicide—I was thankful she talked about it as there was less chance of her doing anything drastic this way than if she had kept it all to herself. I kept all supplies of aspirin (except about half a dozen so that she wouldn't be suspicious and start searching) hidden in my room.

The extraordinary thing about all this was that she could appear more or less normal with other people, and it was only I who really saw how she was. At the peak of this crisis Alice and Julie came to tea with us. Everything went quite as usual until the evening and then the other two joined up in some little game. In any case Pam had gone downstairs to ride her bicycle so she had brought it on herself but, on returning, she came in to see the two of them playing together and I think she felt completely outside the family circle. She started crying, and they tried to comfort her without success as, of course, they had no idea what was behind the trouble. After they had gone back to the Home she spent a long time on the balcony and then went in to our neighbours. I let her go, hoping that their ever-open ears might relieve the tension, but it came to 10.30 and she was still not home so I tapped on their door. To my amazement she refused to come home, in fact she wouldn't even come to their front door to start with. Eventually she came as far as the landing, and started crying again saying how she hated me and that she was leaving me. She turned towards the stairs. I gave her a sharp command to come in. She came back and slunk past me into our flat. I shut and bolted the door quickly. Then she turned on me. When she had been unhappy in the afternoon with her sisters I had tried to show understanding and sympathy and we talked for some time, after which she seemed a little better. In any case, there had been nothing earlier that day to bring about this sudden hate of me. There was only one thing left—kindness and understanding had not worked, so I turned on her this time, calling her cruel and selfish. I said I had no more to say, and didn't want to hear any more and that she was to go straight to bed. To my shock and relief she was fast asleep within half an hour, and it looked as though nothing had been wrong. In the morning she behaved quite normally, except that she did ask what would happen if she fell over the balcony. I realised then how very near she had been to doing just that the previous evening, so I fobbed her off saying that the most she would do would be to break her leg. During the past twenty-four hours she had been as unbalanced as I had ever seen her. I realised, after this episode, that she would use any method to get sympathy from outsiders, even to the extent of making me look like a brute in their eyes.

She improved a little and we went on fairly steadily for the next few weeks, and now Julie was coming to stay for one or two weekends before her permanent move. When Julie did come for good Pam was very excited and she was very good over many things. We had had several talks about how things would be, so she was prepared (as prepared as she could be). As was to be expected Pam did go backwards to quite a large extent, just as a toddler does at the arrival of a new baby in the family. Then, one day, things boiled up again and this time Pam hit Julie hard on the head, giving her earache. Things were getting out of hand again, and she was blurting out silly hurtful things to Julie so I decided I must have help, otherwise Julie would become a problem, too. After all, she was now suffering the upheaval that Pam had suffered the previous year, and although she was a happy little girl on the surface, it didn't take much to make her feel unwanted. Pam played on this, time and time again saying, 'I wish I never ask you 'ere!' I arranged for Pam to go to London to see her Child Care Officer where she could speak freely, away from the atmosphere that was causing her so much unhappiness, and on the morning of her London trip she left me in a terrible state of mind, in fact I wouldn't have been at all surprised if she hadn't come back. I visualised the Child Care Officer recommending her to move straight into a hostel, and once again I had the deep sense of failure, which stayed with me all day. At about 9.45 p.m., however, she came back home. A miracle had happened. The months-old cloud of depression had lifted, and she walked into the flat a new girl. The Child Care Officer had by no means lectured her. What she did do was take her to visit 'Dad' for the evening. It was a purely social visit, and he hadn't been warned. I suppose this unexpected visit to 'Dad' and the obvious pleasure he showed strengthened her relationship with him and she felt really 'one of the family'—something she hadn't felt since she had known the truth about him. He told her a lot about herself as a small baby, how they had had to put her in the washing basket as they had no cot for her and all these little details about her early days must have brought her great relief.

Who knows what had gone on in her mind all those dreadful months. I know she had worn me down—in fact I was ready to give up; not so much because I couldn't stand it, but because I felt I was doing her no good and that she would be better off in a hostel in London. However, it was all over now, and we moved on into one of the happiest times we had ever had up till then. My only troubles were with Julie, and these were to be expected at this stage. She was still 'testing' me as Pam had done when she first came, but although she could be very naughty indeed, she was alert and interested in everything, and she began to make good headway at school, so I felt there was no very serious trouble there.

Academically Pam was a 'wash-out'. At least that was what I was led to believe by her Headmaster at the E.S.N. school. He had assured me that there was 'nothing more there' and that I would be doing a lot more harm than good if I tried to force her on. I agreed with the latter part of his advice. I had no intention of trying to coach her. Her knowledge was nil, and her reading and writing ability was nil, too (she could copy perfectly, but that was all), so it looked as though there was little hope of her ever learning much; but despite all evidence to the contrary, I had a feeling that the picture was not as black as it was painted, and if only I could get to the bottom of *why* she couldn't do these things, then we might begin to get somewhere.

Once or twice, when she had been caught 'off balance' I had discovered that she was able to read, not only very little words, but some quite unusual ones. She had been as surprised as I was at this revelation. This only happened on very rare occasions, and usually if she was giggling—in effect, when she managed to forget herself completely. Whenever she *tried* to read she seized up mentally at once. In fact, she was suffering from a mental block.

I realised that if she was ever to improve she must begin to experience success, however small, and she must certainly *never* experience failure. The moment she failed at anything she was ready to give up. She had no perseverance, no self-drive (except in her fight of my so-called 'poshness'). It was essential then, that I put only success in her way, and I began to protect her even more from all possible forms of failure, both in relationships with people, and in her own endeavours. One of her first real successes was a pullover she knitted for herself. Of course she couldn't read the pattern and she took all the instructions from me verbally—a very tedious experience when shaping the shoulders and neck edge! However, we succeeded between us, and she completed and wore a pullover that she had made single handed, apart from some fairisle that I put in at the bottom to make it more interesting.

She had done well at cooking while she was at school, but she didn't show much interest in this at home, although I tried to encourage her. Having been the servant of all while she was in the Home—it was the only way she could get attention or make friends there—she became excessively lazy with me. In a way I suppose it was flattering, because I was the first person she dared to treat in this new way. Even her bedroom was a disgrace. One would have expected her to take a real pride in the first bedroom she had ever had to herself, but it didn't work like that. So, unfortunately, I wasn't able to use any form of domestic work as a stepping-stone to success at that stage, although this was her natural bent.

Throughout this time I was watching and waiting for an opportunity which would bring her real success, perhaps enabling her to do something many other people couldn't do, thus giving her ego a tremendous boost.

My answer came many, many months later when I was taking her to a summer fête. She had two or three sixpenny rides on a horse. Although she wasn't dressed for riding, I could see that she would look well on a horse. She was scared the first time, but a handsome youth was in charge of her horse and this was an added attraction and she took courage. At the time horse riding seemed out of the question, but I kept the idea at the back of my mind. It was not easy to imagine her out with a class of young ladies taking riding lessons—she would not have been at all at home in that sort of company—on the other hand I could certainly picture her on a horse.

Things always fit into place if you are only ready to jump at opportunities when they present themselves, and an opportunity did come along after yet another long wait. I heard of a stable several miles away which was far from 'posh'—no jodhpurs required, a very reasonable price, and what is more we managed to arrange individual lessons for Pam and my cousin, who was also very keen to learn. Pam and Mary had always got on well together, despite the years between them, but they now began to form a real friendship. They left home at 7.30 one Sunday morning and went in Mary's car to the stable.

In the past, one of my ways of protecting Pam was to warn people with whom she would have to come into contact about her difficulties so that they could limit their vocabulary to small words to avoid her misunderstanding them and also to warn them against showing any form of shock at her behaviour, which was still very unpredictable. However, on this occasion I decided to see how she would get on with the riding instructress without me 'explaining her away'. She was starting something completely fresh, and there was no reason why she should fail, particularly as there would only be the three of them involved in the lesson, Pam, Mary and the girl teaching them.

She returned from the first lesson radiant. She had done well —better, in fact, than Mary who had had a certain amount of difficulty in getting on the horse, and so she was very pleased with herself indeed. At last here was something she could do as well, if not better, than someone else.

By sheer coincidence, Pam had received a letter from my father the day before. As she hadn't asked for help in reading it I assumed that she hadn't attempted to do so. I can claim no merit for my knowledge of psychology for the next part of my story. As she walked in from riding, I remembered the letter and said that if she hadn't read it, perhaps she had better get it quickly in case there was a message for me. She went straight to her room and brought it out, but instead of handing it to me as she usually did, she stood in the hall, with the three of us round her, while she read it aloud— fluently. I think I stepped in quickly with two or three words to save her hesitating and giving up, and she read a full-page letter with understanding for the first time in her life. When she had finished she looked stunned and even more radiant. The miracle had happened. She had read fluently and what is more, with witnesses, who would be able to remind her of her success if more difficult times lay ahead. We were turning the corner at last.

With a girl like this, who had suffered so many rejections and failures, this one great success was not sufficient to enable her to read fluently all the time, and for a long time she went on as before, as if the miracle had never happened. Her reading only became easier when she was full of confidence and this was, needless to say, usually connected with horses. She began to try and read words on the television, and gradually she began to build up a 'permanent' vocabulary—one which remained—despite her moods.

I have said very little about Julie, because it is Pam's story that I am concerned with here, but I think it only fair to Julie to say how well she treated Pam's difficulties. I had hoped that it wouldn't be necessary to tell her, but it became obvious that the more Julie caught up at school (and she needed to catch up, too, as—at ten years old—she was barely able to read), the more she 'showed off' at home and it began to cause friction between the girls. I had told Pam, when we first mentioned Julie joining, that if she kept her mouth shut and her ears open she would learn a lot from Julie who was bound to talk about school. However, the friction started and I was compelled to take Julie to one side and explain to her about Pam's backwardness, and the fact that she had not been able to go to an ordinary school because she couldn't read. I stressed the need for understanding and the fact that Pam was *never* to be laughed at for her shortcomings in this direction. This was hard news for a ten year old, but, to my knowledge, Julie was nothing but helpful in this direction—sometimes too helpful as she tended to step in and read for Pam which was not always good coming from a child seven years her junior; but one warning look from me and Julie would stop.

So at last I had stumbled upon the one thing that was going to 'set her free' from her mental block prison. Week after week went by and I had nothing but good reports of her riding, and with this came little improvements in so many other ways.

There was one minor set-back. She was still working at the rehabilitation centre where she was constantly in contact with people who were severely handicapped, some of them through accidents. She had been riding for some time when they brought a boy into the rehabilitation centre, badly injured through a fall from a horse. This must have played on her mind as her next lesson was a complete failure. She had been frightened, near to tears, and when she came home she was ready to give up. During the lesson, her behaviour had been such that Mary wondered whether it would be wise to tell the instructress of her backwardness. It must have been very obvious. We talked it over, and then I had a word with Pam, pointing out that Jane had never been told and that she was the first person to accept Pam as quite normal, and surely Pam didn't want Jane to have to know now. Couldn't she possibly keep her fear hidden—fear which we all feel from time to time—so that Jane could continue to accept her as normal? She took up the challenge and put up a very brave fight (with herself) the following lesson. And so we crossed yet another very big hurdle —the beginnings of self-control.

I was beginning to be complacent. We had come through many very trying times, but these were becoming fewer and of shorter duration, and months at a time elapsed when we jogged along very happily.

Ever since I had known Pam I had realised that if she was to improve at all she had to learn to trust somebody and from the very beginning I had gone out of my way to let her know that she could trust me. I had accepted the fact that it would take years and years to undo the damage her mother had done and so I was never shocked at her lack of trust, but I still went on, determined never to let her down, whatever the circumstances. I also knew that I would have to maintain a very steady pattern of behaviour myself, being consistent in my reactions to her behaviour as well.

It was impossible for Pam to find a 'middle road' in anything. She was either right up or right down—she loved or hated. She tended to 'bubble' if things were going well, and this bubble had always burst and ended in trouble of some sort. I tried to explain this to her once, suggesting that she should try and harness her feelings and keep them under control.

Having held on to this very stable and secure atmosphere for well over a year, the crash came—on my side. I had been very fortunate as far as my own health was concerned, but in the January I developed a cough which became more and more serious. In the end I had to admit to the girls and myself that I was not at all well, that I would be staying away from work, and that I would need the doctor. I couldn't stay in bed all day as it was very hard to relinquish my household chores entirely, but I did think that Pam would rise to the occasion and be a little more considerate than usual. To my horror, and it was horror, as I was far from well, her reaction was just the opposite. She began to 'play up' and after about a day or so said she was going to leave me. I seemed unable to do or say anything that would make her see sense, and convince her that we would come through this minor upheaval. Of course I realised then my mistake. I had turned myself into her 'rock' in which she had seen no previous (apparent) weakness, and now I was needing to lean on her and she was very frightened. Also this present situation was giving her a 'flashback' into the past and her own family break-up. The initial cause of the mother's desertion was illness and an operation. It was ten-year-old Julie who rallied round and gave me some of the comfort and help I needed. Needless to say this left Pam with a guilt complex which made matters even worse.

It is, perhaps, interesting to mention here that, many months previously, the Child Care Officer had suggested that Pam might settle better if I could show that I needed her and relied on her and that if an opportunity came, I should take to my bed and let her wait on me.

When the opportunity did come, the result was quite the reverse. Far from feeling glad that I needed her, she became terrified. I think a more normal girl would have risen to the occasion and got considerable pleasure from being trusted to take over, but Pam was still so utterly helpless.

I saw now, for the first time, how very heavily she had been leaning on me and to what extent she had come to trust me and I knew how dangerous this was going to be. What would happen to her if I died? She would be worse off than if I had never met her! Of course I was naturally depressed by my illness and I expect I exaggerated the situation, but it gave me time to think and see just what I was achieving, and I wasn't at all satisfied with what I saw. I had turned this girl from a numbed and helpless creature into a 'living' human being who was building up self-confidence to a limited degree; I had protected her so closely from unkindness and misunderstanding from outsiders that for her to imagine life without me was a nightmare. Now I found she could only make progress while I was functioning as her 'tower of strength'. I don't think I had been entirely wrong in the past. She would never have made any progress at all without my protection but I knew then that, if she was to become a 'whole' person, able to live 'under her own steam', I must begin to withdraw myself bit by bit, even to the extent of letting her be hurt by others and experiencing small everyday failures and disappointments the same as everyone else.

My doctor recommended that I should get away for a few days on my own as soon as possible as my cough was being caused partly by nervous tension brought about by Pam's sudden 'collapse'. Apart from one weekend away from them months previously, I had had no break at all. After my first experience of leaving them I had decided that it was easier to plod on rather than suffer, on my return, the emotional upheavals my absence had caused. Anyway, things were more desperate this time so I told Pam that I would be going to my parents for a weekend. She was shocked and distressed at first, but I explained that it was quite normal for a mother to have a weekend away with relatives or friends, so long as her children were in good hands. I explained further that I had every intention of going, and that if the two of them couldn't make a success of such a weekend (planned as it was with my cousin Mary, whom they knew well by now, coming to stay with them so that their routine would remain unchanged) then I would have to make arrangements for them to be sent by the Authorities to a Home of some sort, because I just had to have a rest. After all, House Mothers in Homes have time off work each week, and several weeks' holiday a year away from the children. I think this shocked her, and she became more reasonable. She agreed to the weekend with Mary so it was arranged, and everything went well. My doctor had warned me that I would probably have to repeat this sort of thing several times before Pam and Julie would feel really safe and sure that I would come back to them, so I took the bull by the horns and fixed a week, not too far distant, with a friend. It was arranged that Mary should come and 'keep **Pam** company', while Julie (who could be a real handful when she felt like it) went to a holiday foster home by the sea. Needless to say I always brought them small presents on my return, which I think helped and gave them something to look forward to.

Once again this was a success, in fact my welcome home from Pam was, 'Oh, you 'ome already!' This could have been disconcerting, but I was thrilled. At last she had proved to herself and me that she could carry on and even enjoy life without me. From then on she seemed to shed many of the childish ways. She was much more independent; she began writing letters without showing me—quite often they were to members of her or my family, and they even included letters to 'pop' stars asking for autographs. I did nothing to stop her, and she began to receive replies, proving to her that her writing was intelligible to others.

At this stage she even took one more tremendous step forward, and that was to go away for a weekend by herself with a group of young people. She had no *real* friends of her own making in our home town as she had been such a social misfit, and was quite unable to make a firm friendship—she had nothing to give. Besides, the sort of youngsters to whom she would have been attracted would never have understood her. However, the last thing I wanted was to shut her off from young people, so, when she had first moved in with me, I had arranged with a girl of her own age (but who was completely at the other end of the academic scale) to call in on Friday evenings. Pam was very shrewd and she knew this was a put-up job, but this young girl was a 'brick'. She gave all and received nothing in exchange. Week after week she came, and on many occasions Pam was very rude. Still she came, and eventually included her boyfriend in the visits too; a risky thing to do with Pam around as she always made a bee-line for the boys, neglecting the girls. On one occasion Jennifer confided that she thought Pam was much more interested in her boyfriend than in herself, but still stuck it out. One Friday they asked me if I would mind them asking Pam if she would like to go away for an Easter weekend with them, and about ten others. I jumped at the idea as it was just what she was needing, and tied up so well with my own visits alone. She had stood up to me being away from her, and now here was the opportunity for her to go away from me. She was very hesitant at first, but not adamant, so I put on a little pressure by way of encouragement and she agreed to go. Despite many misgivings, she eventually left, travelling in the back of her 'friends'' car. I never really found out how she behaved while away as I had promised her I had no intention of asking anyone because I felt sure she would behave quite normally. She came back happy, and although she assured me she had no intention of going next year, I am sure she got on quite well, and even enjoyed most of it. I should mention that it was a weekend combining pleasurable seaside pursuits with serious Easter discussions. I even wonder if she contributed at all to the discussions. No doubt her views would have been very enlightening! She certainly came back with a better attitude towards Jennifer and began to talk of her as though she really was her friend.

She was still working at the rehabilitation centre after twelve months there (quite an achievement for a child like this—they usually flit from job to job, but at the first sign of unrest I had put my foot down and said she was to try and stick it out until she was eighteen. There would be things she didn't like in all jobs and it was no good running away every time things went wrong). So, after this twelve months she was feeling quite 'one of them'. Although she was employed for the purpose of washing up, she did come into contact with the patients and even helped with them in small ways if there was a shortage of staff.

It was just before I became ill that Bobby came into the picture. He arrived there as a patient just before Christmas. I think she had been carrying on a mild flirtation with one of the other patients, and had bought him a tie as a present. Then something went wrong with that little romance and within a day she had switched her affections (and the tie) to Bobby. He was nearly twenty-one, and paralysed from the waist down as a result of polio at the age of seven. I didn't really know what to think, so I tried to play for time. I certainly didn't feel I should over-ride her in this sort of thing. She had few enough privileges for a seventeen-year-old as she was always at home, apart from visiting my friend and attending Cubs each week. She had had the one previous experience of 'love' with the Irish boy. I let matters rest for as long as I could, and then I found that Bobby was asking her to go to his home for a weekend. This did present a problem as I couldn't let her sleep away from our home without having the consent of the Child Care Officer, and also it meant that I should meet his parents. How much should I tell them? Pam was still immature and unstable, not to mention almost illiterate, and in any case I couldn't have her rejected yet again. She had been very near suicide the last time. It was arranged for Bobby's parents to come and see me one Sunday afternoon on their way to visiting him. They seemed extremely pleasant people, and very understanding. We talked very frankly, and they still seemed happy for Pam to visit them for a weekend.

It was surprising how much organising was needed one way and another, but she did eventually go, and enjoyed herself as far as I could tell. I was surprised at how critical she had become of other people's behaviour in their homes. I know I had had to be very fussy with her in order to catch up on her original lack of training, but I didn't think we were living at such a high standard!

It was not long after that weekend that she came home from work, telling me that Bobby had asked her to get engaged. I knew she was far from ready for such a step, but felt it would be wrong to ridicule the suggestion, so I said that they would be wise if they kept it a very close secret, just between the two of them, until she was eighteen—that meant a year in which anything could have happened. I was naturally concerned that he was so badly handicapped, but I was very conscious of the fact that it was extremely unlikely that she would ever get a 'normal' man, because she was still so very far from normal herself. I thought that, perhaps, so long as he was a decent, steady boy, she could do very much worse than marry someone like him. In him she had found someone who needed her so badly that he was hardly in a position to reject her, and she would feel secure with him.

His parents seemed very keen on the idea, and, if it is possible, they were pushing their son even more. No doubt they were concerned for his future when they would no longer be able to care for him.

These thoughts I was keeping to myself—I was playing for time as far as Pam was concerned, but I didn't have to wait long. She came home one day and announced that Matron and the physiotherapist had both had a word with her and told her that it was quite out of the question for her to think of marrying Bobby and that he would be going back home. She did not appear all that upset, and she allowed herself to be guided by them. It was a very queer situation. The only indication I had that she had any feelings on the matter at all was that she suddenly started to play with the dolls again. I found them all over the place; sometimes in her bed, sometimes in the washing basket (was this a flashback to the story of herself as a baby?), and she would sit holding one and playing with it all the evening. This was the first time she had had anything to do with them since Julie had moved in. Julie was very good about it. She certainly didn't laugh and she 'gave' her one or two of her own to play with. It lasted about a fortnight. In the end I told her my thoughts on the subject, saying at the same time that, as long as she enjoyed playing with them she could, but that I felt it might help her if she understood why she was doing it. First, I thought it was because she was transferring her love for Bobby to the dolls. She was a very 'dark horse' and who knows what she had really felt for him. Second, I had the feeling that she may have been trying to prove to herself and everyone else that she was still a little girl, and was nowhere near ready for the grown-up world of engagements and marriage.

I think Bobby was more hurt than Pam. On several occasions he tried to contact her by letter, but she allowed herself to be guided by me. I did not forbid her to write, but suggested she should not do so for about a year, in order to give herself time to get to know other people. If she felt like contacting him again in the years to come, and they both wanted to be engaged then, then I for one would do nothing to stand in her way. She accepted this advice and remained quite steady. We certainly didn't have any of the previous trouble after the other broken romance.

Life was beginning to rush her. If she got caught up in a real romance at this point she would probably end up with someone far from normal; if she could only wait a year or two she would doubtless make considerable progress and her tastes and ambitions would be quite different. But how to hold her back in this most natural of progressions until she had reached her full stature in other directions—that was the problem.

Pam was maturing quickly now—one success brought another —until she appeared to be able to maintain an even standard of behaviour. She had little ups and downs, but they were very small in comparison with those of the past, and she soon got over them.

It was my turn to be shocked now as I had no idea she was still 'fermenting' about her real father. Obviously one can't forget things like this completely, but I thought she had accepted the situation.

Ever since January, when she had received a leather writing case for her birthday, she had been writing little letters to family and old school friends without my help. I had tried to keep outside all this so that she could begin to experience privacy. One evening in May she wrote five letters, but I wasn't perturbed, thinking they were in the same vein as her previous correspondence. Imagine my shock when she announced that she had found out who her real father was. She had written twice to her mother, but got no answer, so she wrote to her coloured brother, asking him to go and see the mother and try to get the information. She met him at the Home one Sunday and he told her the news. Even then she kept it to herself for two whole weeks, and her behaviour on the surface was perfectly normal.

She told me she was satisfied now (her real father was her own uncle by marriage, whom she knew) and that although she didn't like him all that much, it was far better to know who you were, than to live in perpetual doubt. This presented a tricky problem as it was now quite obvious why the mother hadn't told her the truth in the first place. It was very likely that even the uncle himself didn't know he was her father, let alone 'Dad', and it would cause chaos if this information reached their ears. Pam was more concerned for her own brothers and sisters—she felt they had the right to know about her. I advised her to say nothing, as we had discussed this matter before and felt there was no need for them to know, but I did say that if she really felt she had to, then she must start by telling Julie, and to let me know when she did so that I could 'step in and pick up the pieces' if necessary.

I think, once again, that by 'opening all the doors' and making it possible for her to tell Julie, it held her back. Maybe they will be told one day but I think that Pam will now grow so accustomed to the idea of knowing who she really is, that she will not feel the need to tell the others.

Once again the Child Care Officers had been proved right in saying that these children must not be shut off from the past, much as it appeared to hurt them. If I had interfered at all during this time I am sure I would have done a great deal of damage in my ignorance; as it was, Pam ferreted out the information for herself, was composed throughout, and when she felt able to talk to me about it she did so. It is the easiest thing in the world to assume all is going well if the children appear quite happy, but one must never ignore the possibility of underlying anxieties nor do anything to frustrate their efforts to resolve them.

I find it almost impossible to bring my story of Pam to a satisfactory conclusion as, of course, there is no ending; we are really only at the beginning now as she emerges from the darkness of distrust, despair and helplessness. Even as I have been writing I could have added many more incidents as there is constant change, but I think it is time to call a halt and collect my wits to see just what has happened during the past two years.

Several big questions present themselves to me. One that causes me most concern is this. Is it right to break up a family such as the one my girls come from? Much thought was given to this before I started this venture and it was decided that, under such circumstances, if an opportunity came for only one, then it still must be taken. Having taken the opportunity the next problem presents itself. Is it better for the children, given the new home in a new environment, to break completely from the past and their families, finding new friends and a new way of life; or is it better for them to be kept in touch with all that is so degrading, and of which they will grow to be ashamed as they experience the new way of life and mix with children from ordinary, happy families? I know the answer the Child Care Officer gives me is really the right one, but it is very hard to carry out. From their years of experience they feel it is right for the children to grow up in touch with both worlds so that the final choice of way of life shall be their own, and not forced upon them by 'people who know better'. I do agree really, but it is agony to see your children being hurt by this constant reminder of the past. I have deliberately given Pam access to both her parents and her brothers and sisters. Her mother let her down yet again after her visit to us. Her sister, Jean, frequently lets her down and causes her great anxiety over the baby which she is finding it more and more difficult to cope with. Alice and Johnny are always at loggerheads with my two, mainly because their way of life in the Children's Home is inevitably so different—even accents are beginning to be different, particularly with Julie who is at school in this area. I am not trying to force my two to become 'little ladies', but if this place is going to become their home and they feel at one with the people around them, then they must raise their standards and come to understand what our sort of family life is like. As for the youngest boy, Ronnie (and apart from Jean who saw him on the one occasion mentioned), they haven't seen him since he was a baby over seven years ago. He doesn't know of their existence, but a week hardly goes by without him being mentioned by them. If there is any form of family unrest, then he becomes even more real to them and they long for him. Apart from having to see my girls hurt by all these family connections, I also have to become involved with their real family myself which can lead to all sorts of complications.

I long for the day when Children's Homes, as we know them today, can be abolished, being substituted for by many more foster homes or very small Children's Homes (an ordinary house in an ordinary road). I know this idea isn't original and that experiments are already being made in this direction. To take already desperately unhappy children and herd them together in large communities cannot help them really; apart from creating more problems in turning them into one of a large community and all that that means, it cannot possibly give help where their need is greatest—it merely provides shelter until they are eighteen, and then the world is even more unkind.

I wish more single women could know that it is possible for them to foster children. It is a question of adapting one's employment to meet the needs of the child as far as possible, but this can be done. It means living a very full life and probably sacrificing some of the old pastimes and pleasures, but the rewards so far outweigh the sacrifices that they cease to be sacrifices. It could be said that it is wrong for a mother (or foster mother) to be working full time, and of course it isn't ideal from many points of view. On the other hand, I am sure it has helped to establish a real bond of trust between Pam, Julie and me, because I really do have to trust them for about an hour each day before I arrive home from work. They have each other's company, and very often I come home to find one or other of them (usually Julie) has done some housework for me so that I can rest a little more in the evenings. Naturally I reward their efforts in some small way, but I think it has helped them to feel that it is really their own home. I also think that, for a single person, some sort of employment is necessary. One of the things I miss most is adult company and conversation, and I don't think I could have struggled on sometimes if I hadn't been able to leave home behind and have an interesting job to go to. It enables me to 'get outside' our troubles and come home refreshed.

I must finish by saying that I couldn't even have begun this venture without the encouragement and strong backing of all my family and friends, and last but not least, the Child Care Officers. Although I am a single woman, living alone with these two children, I am by no means really alone and I could have done nothing without them all.

References

Beker, J. (1965) 'Male adolescent inmates' perceptions of helping persons', *Social Work*, 10 (2), pp. 18-26.

Butrym, Z. (1968) *Medical Social Work in Action*, Occasional Papers on Social Administration No. 26, Bell.

Cohen, A. (1972) 'The consumer's view: retarded mother and the social services', *Social Work Today*, 1 (12), pp. 39-43.

George, V. (1970) *Foster Care: Theory and Practice*, Routledge & Kegan Paul.

Goldberg, E. M. (1970) *Helping the Aged*, Allen & Unwin.

Goodacre, I. (1966) *Adoption Policy and Practice*, Allen & Unwin.

Gottesfeld, R. (1965) 'Professionals and delinquents evaluate professional methods with delinquents', *Social Problems*, 13, pp. 45-59.

Mayer, J. E. and Timms, N. (1970) *The Client Speaks*, Routledge & Kegan Paul.

Meyer, J. H., Borgatta, E. F. and Jones, W. C. (1965) *Girls at Vocational High*, Russell Sage Foundation.

Nicholson, J. (1966) *Mother and Baby Homes*, Allen & Unwin.

Oakeshott, M. (1955) 'The customer is never wrong', *Listener*, 25 August, pp. 301-2.

Schmidt, J. T. (1969) 'The use of purpose in casework practice', *Social Work*, 14 (1), pp. 77-84.